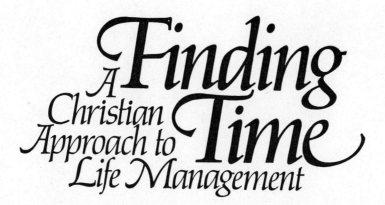

A Christian Approach to Finding Time
Life Management

Rick Yohn

WORD BOOKS
PUBLISHER
WACO, TEXAS

A DIVISION OF
WORD, INCORPORATED

Library of Congress Cataloging in Publication Data

Yohn, Rick.
  Finding time.

  Bibliography: p.
  1. Time management—Religious aspects—Christianity.
2. Christian life—1960–   I. Title.
BV4598.5.Y64   1984   248.4   83–23469
ISBN 0–8499–0374–2

Printed in the United States of America

CONTENTS

PART I

MAKING TIME WORK FOR YOU, RATHER THAN AGAINST YOU

1

Time—Never Enough of It

Introduction

It may be the student writing an exam paper; a housewife, talking on the phone while she cooks supper and watches her two-year-old waddle across the floor with a special fragrance trailing behind; or a businessman working into the wee hours of the night. All express the same frustration: *I need more time.*

My own time management problems began early in my life. Brought up in the radio era as a young child, I loved staying up to hear Red Skelton, "Fibber McGee and Molly," "Bulldog Drummond," "Lights Out," "Mr. District Attorney," and other programs. Since many of those programs aired past my bedtime, it was a routine knock-down-and-drag-out between my parents and myself. Sometimes they'd compromise by turning up the volume, so that I could lie in my bed and listen intently, as the sound-effects crew made the stories come alive. I believe that's when I first developed my interest in sound effects: creaking door, shooting, ship setting sail, and so forth.

Later I had trouble managing to get home on time from sledding in the park during the cold, Pennsylvania winters. I enjoyed playing in the snow so much that I'd completely forget time. Then in my teen years there were the hassles of being home on time after a date. Yes, as the years have passed, my time management has been an uphill battle!

In my roles as a student, a husband, a father, a pastor, and a writer, using my time wisely is a constant challenge, and with all of the books and seminars focusing on time management, the problem is obviously widespread. Let's look at this thing that we call *time*. What is time, anyway?

R. Alex MacKenzie says that time is a *unique resource*. In his book *The Time Trap,* he writes, "It cannot be accumulated like money or stockpiled like raw materials. We are forced to spend it, whether we choose to or not, and at a fixed rate of 60 seconds every minute" (p. 2). Edward Dayton claims that time is no more than a *rhythm of events*. In *Tools for Time Management,* he writes, "Early man measured time by the rising of the sun or the moon. Modern man measures time with the use of atomic clocks. But whether it be the using of the sun or the motion of the atom, it is still event upon event" (p. 175).

Alan Lakein takes time more seriously believing that "Time is life. It is irreversible and irreplaceable. To waste your time is to waste your life, but to master your time is to master your life and make the most of it" (*How to Get Control of Your Time and Your Life,* p. 1).

And that's exactly what most people want to do—*master* their time rather than be mastered by it. The apostle Paul said it well when he wrote, "Therefore, be careful how you walk, not as unwise men, but as wise, making the most of your time, because the days are evil" (Eph. 5:15–16).

The reason so many of us feel we don't have enough time is that we fail to manage the time we do have. We've developed sloppy habits of time management over the years. In fact, we waste a lot of our time.

Therefore, let's first concentrate on the major causes of our wasting time and what to do about them.

Failure to Understand and Adopt Certain Basic Truths about Time

The first major time waster is our failure to understand and adopt certain basic truths about time for our lives.

We all have the same amount of time but use it differently.

Everyone of us has the same 24 hours in a day, and 168 hours in the week, but we do not all use those hours in the same way, or for the same purpose. In any given hour of the day, the entrepreneur may be closing a million-dollar deal; the housewife may be completing her house chores; the student may be deciding when to get started on his homework; and the man in prison may be staring out his cell window daydreaming of freedom. It's the very same hour of the day, but only the entrepreneur and housewife are using that hour to accomplish anything productive.

Consider the biblical examples of Methuselah and Jesus Christ. We are told that Methuselah lived 969 years, and he died. He had more hours in a lifetime than any other man on this planet—but what did he accomplish during his life? Apparently there was nothing significant enough to record for posterity.

In contrast, Jesus Christ lived only thirty-three years. It was only during His last three years that the Lord made a significant contribution to mankind—but think of His productivity during those three short years. He turned many people away from a life of enslavement to sin. He healed the sick; raised the dead; gave sight to the blind; trained a core group of disciples who, in a few years, turned the world upside down.

The difference between the Lord and Methuselah, among other things, was His use of time. Jesus was never in a hurry. Even when a servant rushed up to Him and told Him about His sick friend Lazarus, Jesus did not rush to Lazarus's side.

He remained at the same place for two more days before travel-ing to Bethany.

The Lord was very conscious of time. He was aware that He had only a short amount of time to accomplish His purpose on earth. Jesus told His brothers on one occasion, ". . . My time is not yet at hand . . . " (John 7:6). Again He said, "Go up to the feast yourselves; I do not go up to this feast because My time has not yet fully come" (John 7:8). However, at another period, Jesus told His disciples, ". . . Go into the city to a certain man, and say to him, 'The Teacher says, "My time is at hand; I am to keep the Passover at your house with My disciples" ' " (Matt. 26:18).

When we use time, we are choosing one activity and excluding another.

It's not how much time you have available, but what you do with your time that is important. A second basic truth, which we often neglect to incorporate into our lives, is that when we use time we are choosing one activity and excluding another.

We tell ourselves, *I'd like to read more books. I need to spend more time studying the Bible. I know that I should spend more time with my kids, but. . . .* If we choose to watch TV, then we are choosing not to read a book, spend time with our children, or do our homework with total concentration. If we choose to spend time with God in prayer, then we have chosen not to watch TV, play a game with the kids, or cut the grass.

The Scriptures provide an excellent illustration of two sisters who, in the same period of time, made two different choices as to how they would use that time. Luke records the event. "Now as they were traveling along, He entered a certain village; and a woman named Martha welcomed Him into her home. And she had a sister called Mary, who moreover was listen-ing to the Lord's word, seated at His feet. But Martha was distracted with all her preparations . . ." (Luke 10:38–40).

This scene is typical in many homes. One sister is an activist. As soon as this special visitor comes into her home, she feels obligated to do something for Him. She wouldn't think of just sitting and talking to Him. She must *do* something.

Then there is the other sister who is content to let the first sister scurry around the kitchen and prepare the evening meal, while she entertains the visitor by listening intently to what He has to say. We can all identify somewhat with these sisters. Many of us are one of these two personality makeups. The psychologists refer to them as the Type *A* and Type *B.*

The Type *A* personality is: (1) *ambitious;* (2) *aggressive;* (3) *self-demanding;* (4) *competitive;* (5) *pushing to be successful;* (6) *driven by the clock.* He's the horn-honker who gets white knuckles when the light turns green and the car in front of him doesn't move. Many top executives, athletes, and managers fall into this category.

The Type *B* personality is: (1) *more casual;* (2) *less competitive;* (3) *less worried about time;* (4) *not so preoccupied by achievement.* This is the man who never seems to be in a hurry. When confronted by problems, he takes them in stride. It's the mother who has five youngsters yelling and screaming at the top of their lungs, while she calmly meets their needs one at a time.

Well, Martha was the go-getter, the high achiever—but Mary had other priorities. She used this time to learn. While Jesus was speaking to Mary, Martha came barging into the room, and interrupted the conversation as she complained, " 'Lord, do You not care that my sister has left me to do all the serving alone? Then tell her to help me' " (Luke 10:40). A typical reaction of the Type *A* personality. They get overburdened with responsibility and very frustrated when others don't appreciate everything they are doing. The normal reaction is to vent their frustration by condemning others who are not as active as they are. Their perspective of others is usually that everyone else is just lazy—a bunch of losers.

Notice, however, Jesus' response to Martha's frustration. He replied, " 'Martha, Martha, you are worried and bothered by so many things; but only a few things are necessary, really only one; for Mary has chosen the good part, which shall not be taken away from her' " (vv. 41–42). He first points out Martha's problem with priorities. Everything in life is *not* of equal importance. However, when you attempt to inform a perfectionist that everything does not have to be perfect, you'll generate an argument.

The second problem that Jesus revealed to Martha was her condemnation of Mary. Therefore, He complimented Mary for what she was doing. Intent listening is not passive. It is quite active. Likewise, prayer, studying Scripture, and reading good books are not passive. They are means of learning and growing.

The third contrast that Jesus made was the difference in the sisters' choice of activity. Martha chose an activity which would provide for nourishment of the body, while Mary chose an activity which would provide nourishment for the spirit. In pointing out this contrast, Jesus was not implying that cooking meals was unspiritual; rather He was saying that there are those times that one needs to set aside for spiritual nourishment and not feel obligated always to focus on food for the body.

When we spend time to feed our souls, we are choosing not to feed our stomachs. The choice that Mary made was an excellent choice, because the time to learn from the Master Teacher was available then.

Doing anything well takes time.

A third important truth to consider about time is that doing anything well takes time. We live in an instant society. Everyone wants everything immediately, if not sooner. We drink instant coffee, eat instant potatoes, instant breakfast, instant pudding, and then get instant indigestion and go on an instant diet.

God is never in a hurry. Everything He does is on a time schedule, but man finds it difficult plugging into God's perspective of time. The apostle Peter illustrates man's misunderstanding of God's view of time. He writes:

> Know this first of all, that in the last days mockers will come with their mocking, following after their own lusts, and saying, "Where is the promise of His coming? For ever since the fathers fell asleep, all continues just as it was from the beginning of creation". . . . But do not let this one fact escape your notice, beloved, that with the Lord one day is as a thousand years, and a thousand years as one day.
>
> 2 Peter 3:3–4,8

The Lord will return to earth when He is ready, and not one day earlier.

Jesus spent thirty years preparing for three years of ministry. The apostle Paul spent many years after his conversion, preparing for his ministry to the Gentiles.

Someone has wisely asked, "If you don't have time to do something right the first time, when will you have the time to do it over?"

After the resurrection of Jesus, His disciples asked Him, " '. . . Lord, is it at this time you are restoring the kingdom to Israel?' " The disciples had been frustrated earlier when their king had been taken and put to death. All of their dreams were shattered, as the spikes were pounded into Jesus' hands and feet. If the king is dead, the kingdom is also gone. But now the king is alive once again. This must be the time to enter into the kingdom. Not so. Jesus had other plans for His disciples, and those plans would not be even initiated for another fifty days.

We need to tune into God's timing for the work that He wants to accomplish. When it is finished, then it will have been done well. If we panic and run ahead of His scheduling in order to be active, we will lose out on His best. And that includes building buildings, starting new churches, or moving a church from one place to another. Doing anything well takes time—and that time must be on God's schedule.

Some things don't get done due to lack of interest, not lack of time.

This is a fourth principle to consider about time. Often when we say, "I just don't have the time," we really mean, "I'm not that interested to take the time." Now there is nothing necessarily wrong with that!

Many men enjoy playing golf. They spend hours on the golf course running after a little white ball that has a great deal of trouble finding a little hole five hundred yards away. I've played golf over the years and have enjoyed it tremendously at times—and hated it with a passion at other times. Today, however, I experience difficulty finding the time to play golf, because my interest level in that sport is relatively low. However, I do find sufficient time to jog.

The nation of Israel spent several months rebuilding the temple. Then they experienced tremendous pressure from the surrounding people to cease their building program. Soon they stopped it completely and just couldn't seem to find the time to get the project started again.

God reminded them through the prophet Haggai, " 'Thus says the Lord of hosts, 'This people says, "The time has not come, even the time for the house of the Lord to be rebuilt." Then the word of the Lord came by Haggai the prophet saying, 'Is it time for you yourselves to dwell in your paneled houses while this house lies desolate?' " (Hag. 1:2–4). They were not involved in God's work due to lack of interest, not lack of time.

When we fail to incorporate into our lives these basic facts about time, we will waste a lot of time by neglecting what we should do and immersing ourselves in activities which keep us from spending time in the important areas of life.

Wasting Time When We Overcommit Ourselves

A major time-waster is that of overcommitment. Two reasons why we overcommit ourselves is that (1) we feel indispensable; and (2) we just don't know how to say *no.*

Some people feel indispensable.

The person who tells himself, *The only way anything gets done around here is for me to do it myself,* usually winds up feeling indispensable. His perspective may be accurate for a number of reasons.

Only one committed. He may be the only person so committed to a certain task that he has to do it himself. Some individuals are excellent idea people. They dream dreams. They can visualize the finished product. They are able to see how all the pieces of the puzzle need to fit. They begin the project and attempt to rally some interest from others for support. But when all is said and done, they are the ones who spend most of the time and energy to complete the task. When this attitude becomes part of their life style, they usually overcommit themselves, feeling that they are indispensable in every project.

Doesn't delegate. A second reason why he or she may feel indispensable is that he doesn't know how or doesn't want to delegate responsibility to others.

Maybe he wants the satisfaction of doing the job himself; or perhaps he is convinced that he can do the task better than anyone else. Whatever the reason, he involves others only to the extent that they support his views or carry out the minor responsibilities. Because the other people are not challenged to accept major responsibilities, they soon lose interest, knowing that it's a one-man operation.

Moses is a good case in point. I do not know why he had failed to involve others at this point of his life, but he was burning himself out in the process. When he was out in the wilderness with the Israelites, his father-in-law, Jethro, paid him a visit. Jethro observed all of the work Moses was doing, and asked:

> ". . . What is this thing that you are doing for the people? Why do you alone sit as judge and all the people stand about you from morning until evening?" And Moses said to his father-in-law, "Because the people come to me to inquire of God . . . and I judge between a man and his neighbor, and make known the statutes of God and His laws." And Moses' father-in-law said to him, "The thing that you are doing is not good. You will surely wear out, both yourself and these people who are with you, for the task is too heavy for you; you cannot do it alone."
>
> Exodus 18:14–18

It's worth noting that some people in this category are unaware of the dangers which generate from doing everything themselves. They don't realize until it's too late how their overcommitment affects them physically, emotionally, and spiritually. They eventually burn out and sometimes never get involved in important tasks after the exhaustion. Others become so frustrated in what they are doing that they yell and scream at everyone who doesn't fall in line properly. Soon the morale is at an all-time low. Everyone becomes edgy. And those with short fuses, blow.

What was Jethro's proposal to remedy the problem? Delegation? Yes! But *wise* delegation. Jethro replies:

> "Now listen to me: I shall give you counsel, and God be with you. You be the people's representative before God, and you bring the disputes to God, then teach them the statutes and the laws, and make known to them the way in which they are to walk, and the work they are to do."
>
> vv. 19–20

Delegate to free yourself to do what you do best.   Here Jethro is setting priorities for Moses (another time-waster is lack of priorities, which we will discuss later). Moses' first and greatest responsibility is to prevent a lot of problems by informing the people of God's law. He was spending all of his time *correcting* the problems rather than *preventing* the problems. Both tasks are important, but since God gave the law to Moses, he was the best qualified to mediate between the people and God, and to teach the people what God required of them.

Delegate to qualified people.   Jethro continues, "Furthermore, you shall select out of all the people able men who fear God, men of truth, those who hate dishonest gain; and you shall place these over them, as leaders of thousands, of hundreds, of fifties and of tens" (v. 21).

Don't delegate responsibilities to just anyone. Some people who think that they are delegators are nothing more than abdicators. They unload responsibility on anyone who is available, or on whomever they can con into accepting the responsibility. Then they abdicate by walking away from the person, never to return, unless a major problem arises. This causes tremendous discouragement among those individuals who are saddled with responsibilities and have nowhere to turn for help.

Delegation needs to be directed toward qualified individuals. Note the threefold qualification: (1) people with the ability to perform the task well; (2) people who have an intimate relationship with God; and (3) people who have an excellent track record, who are known for their honesty and integrity.

There are those who have great ability, but do not walk closely with the Lord. Others may walk closely with the Lord now, but their track record has not been established. They are novices. Therefore, delegate responsibility to those of ability, character, and an excellent track record.

Delegate both responsibility and authority.   Then Jethro concludes, "And let them judge the people at all times; and let it be that every major dispute they will bring to you, but every minor dispute they themselves will judge . . ." (v. 22).

Sometimes we give people responsibility, but fail to give them the authority to make decisions. They have to know what authority they do have, and what their limitations are. These men were not to come back to Moses for counsel as to how they should advise people. They had complete authority to counsel as they were able.

Some people can't say no.

A second reason why we may overcommit ourselves is that we just don't know how to say *no*. Why can't some people say no to more responsibility? Several reasons come to mind, such as guilt, self-image, and the desire to please.

Consider guilt. I've experienced those emotions of guilt over the years. When I'd be with my family, I felt I should be working. When I spent a lot of time at my job, I felt guilty not spending enough time with my family. If I'm writing, I feel like I should read more; but when I read I want to be writing! And I've discovered that when I feel guilty, I can't concentrate on much of anything.

It's important to distinguish between true and false guilt. *True guilt is the result of violating God's principles.* When we lie, commit immoral acts, cheat, or hurt someone, we feel guilty as God's Holy Spirit convicts us of sin. *False guilt is the result of not measuring up to our own or someone else's standard.* If you've been brought up believing that busyness is a virtue, you'll probably feel guilty if you're not busy.

If your boss tells you that you aren't measuring up to the quotas he has established, you may feel guilty; or perhaps you've set very high standards for yourself but have failed to reach those goals. So you feel guilty. That's false guilt.

Self-image. This is another reason why people have difficulty saying no. Busyness makes some people feel very important.

They're involved in civic and church responsibilities; work hard on the job; always available to plug into some new responsibility, because busyness tells them, "I'm needed"; "I'm important"; "people can't get along without me."

Spiritual status. Some also immerse themselves in church activities because they link overcommitment with spirituality. They don't want to be spectators. They want to serve the Lord—but they confuse activity with spirtuality.

God certainly wants us to get involved in serving Him and helping others. The church already has too many spectators who watch others do the work, but swinging the pendulum to the other side is not the answer. High involvement may actually work *against* one's spiritual growth, because time is taken from developing one's relationship with God and spent on church activity.

Desire to please. This is a fourth reason why some people fail to say *no.* This is often a characteristic of the first child. He wants to please his parents, and as he develops socially, he wants to please others. The individual who wants to please everybody often pleases nobody. Pleasing others can be a virtue if the results will be a true help to them. Paul encourages his readers, "Now we who are strong ought to bear the weaknesses of those without strength, and not just please ourselves. Let each of us please his neighbor *for his good,* to his edification" (Rom. 15:1–2, *italics added*).

However, when we have to compromise our standards, violate truth, or neglect other important responsibilities just to please another person, then it becomes a vice not a virtue. The same one who wrote to the Romans about pleasing others also wrote to the Galatians stating, "For am I now seeking the favor of men, or of God? Or am I striving to please men? If I were still trying to please men, I would not be a bondservant of Christ" (Gal. 1:10). You cannot spend the rest of your life trying to make everybody happy. There are some decisions you'll have to make that will make some very unhappy. And at other times, you'll have to turn down opportunities, and that will make some unhappy.

Conclusion

In the next chapter, we will continue to discuss other time-wasters, but let's quickly review the two stated reasons why we waste a lot of time.

First, that we often fail to accept certain basic truths about time:

1. We all have the same amount of time but use it differently.
2. When we use time, we are choosing one activity and excluding another.
3. Doing anything well takes time.
4. Some things don't get done due to lack of interest, rather than lack of time.

Second, that we waste time because we overcommit ourselves, either because:

1. We feel indispensable.
     or
2. We just don't know how to say *no*.

In light of these facts, how well are you making the most of your time?

2

Do You Know Where You're Going?

Introduction

A number of years ago, our family vacationed back East and spent several days in the Washington, D.C., area. As we drove to Washington from Pennsylvania, we stopped to walk around the grounds at Annapolis where the U.S. Naval Academy is located. By the time we left Annapolis, it was getting late, and we hadn't eaten supper yet. So we decided to find a motel about fifteen miles from Washington, get supper, and then drive into Washington at night.

We found a nice motel up on a hill. From there you could see the lights in the nation's capital. After eating, we sped off to see the great city brilliantly lit. We saw the Lincoln Memorial, the Kennedy Center, the Capitol Building, the Washington Monument, and many other spectacular sights. It made us proud we were Americans. We enjoyed ourselves so much, that we hadn't noticed it was already twelve o'clock. We knew that we had about a twenty-five minute ride back to the motel, so we called it a day, hopped into the car, and drove toward our motel.

As we drove, the boys fell asleep in the back seat, and my wife and I cheerfully rehearsed the sights we had just seen. After about thirty minutes of driving, I started to develop an uneasy feeling. I said, "Shouldn't we be at the motel by now?" My wife agreed, and pulled out the map to be certain we were on course. When she asked me on what route the motel was located, I had no idea. So there we were, at 12:30 A.M., driving at a good speed, but with no idea as to where we were going. Every turn we made was a wrong one, it seemed. It was now about 1:45 A.M., and we were still driving the freeways—at the limit of our frustration level—and still had no idea where we were going. Suddenly my wife had a brilliant idea. She asked, "Doesn't the motel have its address stamped on the key?" *Voilà!* Now that we knew where to go, we just had to decide what route would take us there. At 2:00 A.M., we arrived at our destination.

What a waste of time! And the reason so much time was wasted was simply that *we didn't know where we were going.*

That's how it is often in our daily lives. We get up in the morning; go through the motions of attending school; doing something around the house; or going to work and shuffling papers. When all is said and done, more has been said than done. We remain active. We may even get tired. Then, when we look back on the day, the week, the month, or even the year, we wonder, *What have I accomplished?* And too often we sadly come up with a blank. We accomplish so little, and therefore waste a lot of time because *we don't know where we are going.* Therefore, I want to emphasize the great need for setting goals in our life, so let's first define what we mean by a goal.

What Is a Goal?

In their book *Strategy for Leadership,* Ed Dayton and Ted Engstrom define a goal as "an image or picture of the future." It is a "statement of faith." It is a future event "towards which we can measure progress" (pp. 53–54). Goals focus on the future. They allow us to dream dreams. They help us project our present desires and dreams into future realities.

Joseph dreamed about being in a position of great authority, and thirteen years later, his dream came true. David saw the possibility of building a temple for God, and although he himself did not build it, he gathered the resources for the project, and his son Solomon achieved his father's great goal. Nehemiah saw a tremendous need for rebuilding the walls of Jerusalem. After much prayer and careful planning, he set out to achieve his ambitious goal.

Each of these men began with an idea, a desire, or a need. By faith they saw what could be. Then by work they made it happen. A goal is "a statement of faith, focusing on what could be in the future." But why is it so important to have goals? Isn't it better to live a day at a time and handle matters as they appear? Absolutely not! Goals are essential and keep us from wasting time in a number of ways.

How Do Goals Keep Us from Wasting Time?

Goals motivate us to action.

I feel that those times when I'm bored or discouraged, it's because I've run out of goals, not out of things to do. And when I run out of worthwhile goals, the doing becomes less challenging. Goals are like the markers in a marathon race. They allow us to know how far we've already come and how far we need to go.

Though I've never run a marathon, I have my own markers when I jog. Many times, when I've wanted to stop, I would see those two familiar palm trees about three-quarters of a mile from my house, and just the sight of those trees would give me the motivation to complete my run.

If you feel demotivated today—perhaps drifting along in ambiguity—maybe you need either to review your goals to see whether you're on target, or establish goals so that you have something to aim at.

Goals also keep us from wasting time by helping us know what to do next.

Goals help us make decisions.

We have many opportunities before us in a given week to make purchases, to go places, to accept new responsibilities, and to maintain our day-to-day activities. How are we going to decide what we should accept and what we should reject? Without goals, our decisions will be based upon who or what brings the greatest pressure to bear upon us.

When Lazarus was sick, Jesus decided not to go to him immediately, because the Lord's goal was to raise Lazarus from the dead, not heal him from sickness. Illustration: (though the situations are hardly comparable!) you may be deciding whether you should buy a new car or a used car. Your decision will be easier if you have certain written financial goals. If you want a positive cash flow and don't want to accumulate more debt, you may choose the used car. If you want a tax write-off over the next three years, you may choose a more expensive new car. On the other hand, if you have no financial goals, then you'll probably decide on the spur of the moment based on your feelings, rather than on sound judgment. The question you need to answer is not merely, "Can I afford it?" but, "Which decision will help me to achieve my financial goal best?"

In addition to being excellent motivators and a help in making decisions, goals offer another benefit.

Goals protect us from the tyranny of the urgent.

It's often been said that the important things of life are seldom urgent, and the urgent things are seldom important. The incident of Mary and Martha verifies that claim. Martha became entangled in the urgent matter of preparing a meal for the Lord, while her sister, Mary, focused on the important matter of learning from the Lord. Martha became a victim of the tyranny of the urgent.

We tell ourselves that time with God and our family is important. We believe that building relationships is important. We know that developing our spiritual lives is important, but how much time do we really spend on these essentials of life? Until we transform these beliefs into specific goals, we will continually be victims of this tyranny.

Goals also help measure progress.

Goals keep us from wasting time by showing us how far we've come. Dr. Robert Schuller writes in his book *The Peak to Peek Principle,* "The secret of success cannot be found by sitting in an expensive leather chair in a plush office and dreaming your dreams. The secret of success is to select a goal by finding a need and filling it. Find a hurt and heal it. Find somebody with a problem; offer to help solve it" (p. 31).

It's difficult to develop a sense of fulfillment in life when we are aiming at nothing. When there is nothing by which to measure progress, our time will disappear as mysteriously as money in a poorly managed bank account. We'll wonder, *What am I doing with my life that's worthwhile? What contribution am I making to society? What progress am I making in my own life?* Without clearly defined goals, answers to those questions will evade us like a dog when it's time for his bath.

Goals help control the stress in life.

There is a vital link between wasting time and stress. Dr. E. M. Gherman, one of this country's foremost authorities on stress, says, "Stress is closely linked to the achievement of goals. One of the key ways of reducing time stress is to pay more attention to accomplishments than to the time involved. To work comfortably and effectively, you must establish a workload that you or your subordinates can accomplish reasonably well within the time available" (*Stress and the Bottom Line,* p. 53).

Indeed, goals will help us manage our time more effectively. Nevertheless, we often neglect to establish goals, because either we don't know what kind of goals to set, or we don't know how to set them. Let's consider the types of goals first.

What Kinds of Goals Should We Establish?

We should establish long- and short-range goals.

A short-range goal is usually considered one to be achieved within a year, while the long-range goal may be a year or longer. Dr. Ted Engstrom of World Vision wisely preaches that, "We terribly overestimate what we can do in one year and underestimate what we can do in five" (Leadership, Spring 1982, p. 17).

One's long-range goal as a sophomore or junior in high school may be to go to a specific college. Short-range goals will need to include maintaining good grades and taking the courses needed to prepare for that college. They may also include getting a job, so that one will have some money set aside for his education.

As a mother of teenagers, you may have a long-range goal of investing yourself in some significant job or profession or volunteer work, once the nest empties. Your short-range goals may include taking some adult night-school courses; or going back to school; or developing your skills and knowledge, so that you'll be qualified to pursue the long-range objectives after the kids leave home.

God's long-range goal has been to provide eternal life for all who are willing to receive it. His short-range goals include the birth, ministry, death, and resurrection of His Son; the training and sending forth of witnesses to proclaim the gospel and teach the Word.

Goals should cover various areas of life.

Goals should not only be long- and short-range, but should also cover more than one area.

Physical goals. It's important to keep the body healthy. This is the only one we're going to have in this life. Our goal may be to lose ten or twenty-five pounds. It may include beginning an exercise program, taking up an active sport, such as racquet ball, jogging, swimming, or tennis. We may decide to join an aerobics class or tone the body by lifting weights; or we may aim to start taking certain vitamins, or get to bed one hour earlier, or go for walks at night.

Spiritual goals. If you have not yet decided to establish a personal relationship with Jesus Christ, this should be your number one goal in life. Once you have received Christ into your life, you'll need to establish other spiritual goals, such as a regular quiet time with the Lord when you read Scripture and pray. You may want to develop the ability of witnessing effectively as a long-range goal. Then your short-range goal may include getting involved in a training program that teaches you how to witness by actual on-the-spot experience. You may need to establish the goal of personal involvement in serving the Lord, or discovering and developing your gifts and then using them.

Financial goals. Another important area in which to establish goals is in the management of your money. The goals may include specific amounts that you want to save each month, or give, or invest. It may include specific items you'd like to buy, or perhaps your major goal is to get out of debt. If you have no financial goals, you'll probably never know where your money is going, and continue to live from hand to mouth.

Occupational goals. Where are you going in your career? Where do you want to be in five, ten, or twenty years from now? In what areas would you like to improve in your job?

I established a personal career goal several months ago. I had not been satisfied with my preaching for several years, so I decided to really work at preaching. I wanted (and want) to be biblical, practical, and instructive. I wanted people to understand how down to earth the Scriptures are for today's generation. I wanted God to take my messages, as Jesus took the loaves and fish. I wanted Him to multiply the little that I had and feed the multitudes. Therefore, I developed a plan by which my preaching should be improving over the next few months and years.

You may be thinking about a new career, or a new position in your present job. You may want more responsibility or less responsibility. You may establish the goals of greater efficiency and effectiveness in what you are doing on the job. Perhaps you want to get better organized or desire greater productivity.

Educational goals. Where are you going educationally? Are you finished learning? I certainly hope not! You have a vast choice of educational goals available to you.

Several years ago, I decided to return to the classroom after an absence of thirteen years, to pursue my doctorate. Recently my wife received her master's degree. Twenty-two years had passed since she received her bachelor's degree.

You may want to improve as a mechanic, a salesperson, or an executive. Night courses, weekend seminars, and so forth, help the busy person increase his educational development. Perhaps you'd like to read faster and more effectively. Try a speed reading course; or if you want to improve your ability to work with your hands, try a class in craftwork, painting, or decorating.

Social goals. Are you still growing socially? Are you meeting more people and enjoying them less? Do you expect people to make the first move socially toward you?

Why not set a goal of getting to know more people—of developing some close friendships? In the process of establishing some intimate relationships, you'll be developing a solid support system.

When you set your goals, be sure you include long- and short-range goals, as well as goals which cover a wide area of life and be certain that those goals include certain basic characteristics.

Goals should include these basic characteristics.

They should be specific and measurable. Managing money better is not a goal. It's merely a wishful thought. Deciding to get out of debt by next year is a specific and measurable goal. To lose weight is also a mere wish, but to lose ten pounds in the next three weeks is specific and measurable.

The goal should be attainable. One of the problems we face when setting goals is that we either aim too high or too low (such as losing one pound by next year). It's no challenge. If it's too high, such as to look like Miss America by next week (when you are forty-five years of age and fifty pounds overweight), you'll become discouraged and give up the effort!

The goals should be worthwhile. Many of the things to which we give ourselves in a lifetime hold little lasting value. Therefore, if you want to stay motivated as you strive to achieve your goal, be certain that it is worth all the effort it will take to succeed.

After King Solomon established many goals, including the pursuit of pleasure, fame, money, and women, he evaluated his many accomplishments and concluded, "Thus I considered all my activities which my hands had done and the labor which I had exerted, and behold all was vanity and striving after wind and there was no profit under the sun" (Eccl. 2:11). Be sure that what you pursue in life is worth the price you'll have to pay.

The goals should be written. Again, I quote from Dr. E. M. Gherman, the stress expert, as he talks about the importance of writing goals:

> Writing down goals and objectives brings the future into the present by giving you a clearer view of and perspective on what the desired achievement looks like. There is a mystique about the written word, something committed about the tangible quality of a written list. Keep these goals readily visible, so that you ask yourself daily, "Is what I am doing now moving me closer to one of my goals? Are my methods appropriate for achieving my objectives? Or am I creating stress by fighting the clock and the calendar, instead of making them work for me?" (*Stress and the Bottom Line,* pp. 53–54).

Written goals help me tremendously when I feel that I'm spinning my wheels. I can go back over my goals and see what I've accomplished; where I need to put more effort; and what I need to change.

The goals should be scheduled. If our goals are ever going to be fulfilled, we need to decide when we will begin and when we hope to complete that goal. Because we are procrastinators, a starting and completion time are essential.

The goals should be flexible. Some people become very rigid once they establish a goal. They may become so obsessed with completing the goal that nothing stands in the way, even when the circumstances prove that the pursuit is no longer worthwhile.

We must be sensitive to changing circumstances. Decisions are based upon facts, but once those facts change or new information offers strong evidence in favor of changing course, only the foolish will pursue the original course headlong into oblivion.

Now that we've seen what goals are, why they are important for reducing wasted time, and what kinds of goals we can establish, how are we going to begin?

How Can You Set Good Goals?

Our goals are based upon our values, upon needs that we might have or desires we'd like to fulfill. Therefore, we should begin by making an evaluation.

Evaluate where you are now.

1. What needs do I have? What needs do others have where I might help them?
2. What do I value most in life?
3. What unfulfilled ambitions or dreams do I have?
4. What encouragement have others given me for future goals?
5. What abilities and skills do I want to develop?

Now, take the next step.

Transform a need into a goal.

After you evaluate where you are, turn your need or ambition into a goal. If you are in debt up to your earlobes, you should set a goal of getting out of debt by a certain date. If you always wanted to get more education, establish a goal to return to school by next semester. However, sometimes we begin our goal-setting with great enthusiasm, but within a short time, we run into a lot of obstacles.

Discover the obstacles keeping you from pursuing your goal.

You may want to return to school, but you lack the necessary funds. Then your school may have to become the long-range goal, and acquiring the necessary money your short-range goal.

List the benefits from achieving the goal.

This step will help motivate you to keep on keeping on. Often I begin a project with great gusto. However, as time passes and problems mount, I can get discouraged and begin to wonder, *Why am I knocking myself out for this?*

Then, as I remind myself what this project will be able to accomplish when completed, I get excited all over again. Or, if I fail to see any benefit in the goal, I may change course.

Write down some ways to deal with those obstacles.

Just because you run up against barriers doesn't mean that the goal should be set aside. The apostle Paul always ran into obstacles when he preached and traveled from one town to another. He found that he had to be sensitive to where the people were. He met them on their own turf, without lowering his own personal standards. He testifies how he dealt with various obstacles in 1 Corinthians 9:19–23:

> For though I am free from all men, I have made myself a slave to all, that I might win the more. And to the Jews I became as a Jew, that I might win Jews; to those who are under the Law, as under the Law, though not being myself under the Law, that I might win those who are under the Law; to those who are without law, as without law, though not being without the law of God but under the law of Christ, that I might win those who are without law. To the weak I became weak, that I might win the weak; I have become all things to all men, that I may by all means save some. And I do all things for the sake of the gospel, that I may become a fellow-partaker of it.

Decide on a time to begin and complete your goal.

If you fail to schedule your goals, you'll fail to achieve your goals.

Think about who could help you achieve your goal.

Most of us need the encouragement and support of other people. I would never have written a book, if I had not received support from my family. I never would have completed my doctoral program had my family not backed me completely.

You, too, will need a friend or a group to act as a support system as you strive to achieve some very demanding goals.

Conclusion

One of the outstanding characteristics of God is that He knows where He is going. He has a Masterplan which is composed of many long-range and short-range goals. Each one of those goals is on a timetable, with a starting date and a completion date. God does nothing haphazardly. He is precise in His activity. He makes time work for Him.

If Christ lives in your life, then you are a child of God and you need to begin acting like God does in the use of your time. You can begin right now by deciding beforehand what it is you want to accomplish with your life.

Where are you going? Only you can answer that. And you alone, by God's grace and wisdom, can make it happen.

3

Tomorrow, I'll Get Organized

Introduction

When I was a boy, I was fascinated by trains. My home was just a few blocks from the railroad, so it wasn't unusual to observe the housewives in the neighborhood rush to remove their wash from the clothesline on windy days. That's when black smoke, filled with soot, belched from the steam engines and was carried by the wind over the backyards, preparing to descend on the drying wash.

I also carry fond memories of the times when I would go to my grandmother's house in the country. As I'd lay my head on the pillow, I could hear the evening train, whistling in the distance, as it passed behind her house. It moved so swiftly and with such grace. They were sounds of adventure and travel.

The really special times occurred when we could go to the railroad station and await friends or relatives who would visit us. Standing on the crowded platform, I could see the bright light on the train, even though it was still miles away. As it would approach the station, the train seemed to grow larger. Then with a thunderous roar, the huge engine would pass by in front of me, screeching its wheels and venting its steam.

Finally, it slowed to a complete stop. The train would remain stationary for about five to ten minutes. Then the conductor would call out, "All aboard!" With a sign from the conductor, the engineer released the brake and started the powerful engine on its course.

However, the train did not pull away quickly from the station. It would jerk, spin its wheels, and slowly pull away from the platform, as it tried to overcome the initial inertia. That's why you could (literally) run and catch the train. Even though so much energy was being exerted in its attempt to leave the station, the results of that expended energy were insignificant at first. Once that initial inertia was overcome, the train once again moved with speed, splendor, and grace.

In some ways people are like those old locomotives. They have a tough time getting started on doing what they should do. Once they get moving, however, nothing seems to stop them. The problem of not getting started is called *procrastination*. It's putting off action until some more convenient time, which often never arrives.

Do you find that you are always late for appointments? Do you operate on a rush-only basis, because you've waited until the last minute to get started and have gotten everyone else uptight because they can't meet your rush schedule? Do you find that you live in a dream world of great intentions, but just never seem to find the time to begin any worthwhile project? Are you in the habit of staying up late to do homework, study for an exam, or to prepare papers for your boss tomorrow? If you meet any of these criteria, you qualify as a procrastinator. If you don't meet these criteria, you're still probably a procrastinator.

Why do we put things off? How can we break that habit and get ourselves on a proper schedule, so that we aren't always being rushed? This chapter will deal with both of these questions. The first focus is on the whys of procrastination.

Why Do We Procrastinate?

Fear.

One of the most common reasons why we procrastinate is fear. The fear of confrontation; the fear of failure; the fear of reality; or even the fear of the unknown, can paralyze us to the point of indecision and passiveness.

One area in which many people procrastinate concerns their health. Statistics reveal that the average woman waits six months before going to a doctor when she discovers a lump. Thousands of people put off going to the dentist because they fear pain. Others put off going to church because they fear that the reality of sin will confront them.

Felix was a case in point. As governor of Judea, Felix heard the apostle Paul defend himself against his accusers. The Book of Acts records the event:

> But some days later, Felix arrived with Drusilla, his wife who was a Jewess, and sent for Paul, and heard him speak about faith in Christ Jesus. And as he was discussing righteousness, self-control and the judgment to come, Felix became frightened and said, "Go away for the present, and when I find time, I will summon you."
>
> Acts 24:24–25

That's procrastination resulting from fear.

Laziness.

Another cause of procrastination is laziness.

There is enough laziness in all of us for the writer of Proverbs to ask, "How long will you lie down, O sluggard? When will you arise from your sleep? A little sleep, a little slumber, a little folding of the hands to rest" (Prov. 6:9–10). Normally I'm an afternoon or early-evening jogger. When the summer heat rises, though, I consider jogging in the early-morning hours. So I set my alarm and have all good intentions of getting up to run at the sound of the alarm. And that's when this proverb hits home. The alarm shrills on schedule, but I turn it off, roll over, and go back to sleep, convincing myself that I'll start jogging tomorrow morning.

It's easy to develop a set of good intentions. But once you begin counting the cost, laziness sets in, and tomorrow never arrives.

Lack of direction and plan.

The lack of direction and a clear plan also prevents many from taking affirmative action. Direction answers the question "Where am I going?" while planning explains, "How will I get there?" I find it quite easy to procrastinate when I have to repair something around the house. Not being much of a handyman, I'll find any excuse to get out of fixing a problem. I procrastinate because I usually don't know what to do, nor do I know how to get started. So when the sink in our bathroom clogged, I just ignored it. As the weeks passed, the collection of material in the pipes meshed so tightly that the water would take fifteen minutes to drain. I decided to try a drain de-clogger, which cut the seepage time down to about ten minutes. In a few weeks, though, the sludge collected once again, and the sink filled with slow, seeping water. In desperation, I decided to settle the problem once and for all. Using a Roto-Rooter type of tool, I unclogged that crazy sink in about ten seconds and was shocked at the ease of the job. I envisioned having to take the entire sink apart and spending hours on the project. All I had to do was unscrew the stop, lift it out, run the instrument through the sludge, twist a little, and "voilà!" The sink was fixed. I was so exhilarated over my success that I just can't wait until it gets clogged again, because now I know what I need to do and how to do it.

Perfectionism.

Another reason people procrastinate is that they are perfectionists at heart.

The perfectionist doesn't want to try anything until he knows exactly how everything will work. If there is any possibility of failure or malfunction, he will withhold taking action. He wants no one to see the kinks in his armor. To fail is to lose face. Therefore, to prevent the possibility of any potential problems, he will hesitate until he is satisfied of a fail-safe system or product.

Interestingly, Jesus was perfect, but He was not a perfectionist. He always worked with imperfect people. He operated within an imperfect religious system and established an imperfect church. You have about as much chance to succeed in developing a perfect program or system as you do in ironing a rubber band. There will always be a kink, a bend, or a wrinkle somewhere. Murphy's Law says it best, "Whatever can go wrong, will go wrong." So strive for excellence, but don't waste your time and energy on perfectionism.

Overload.

Did you ever turn on an iron or hair dryer, or plug in an electric skillet and find yourself suddenly without any power? That's overload. When the circuits in your house are drained of too much current, the circuit breaker trips, and your electricity ceases to flow.

Busy people often go into overload. They disperse their energies in so many directions that their circuit blows, and this can lead to anger, frustration, stress overload, or a nervous breakdown. The body screams out, "Stop! It's enough. I can't take any more."

Moses went into overload when the people whom he delivered from Egypt expressed little appreciation, but loudly vocalized their frustrations. When Moses heard their complaints, he cried out to God:

> "Why hast Thou been so hard on Thy servant? And why have I not found favor in Thy sight, that Thou hast laid the burden of all this people on me? Was it I who conceived all this people? Was it I who brought them forth, that Thou shouldst say to me, 'Carry them in your bosom as a nurse carries a nursing infant, to the land which Thou didst swear to their fathers?' Where am I to get meat to give to all this people? For they weep before me, saying, 'Give us meat that we may eat!' I alone am not able to carry all this people, because it is too burdensome for me. So if Thou art going to deal thus with me, please kill me at once, if I have found favor in Thy sight, and do not let me see my wretchedness."
>
> Numbers 11:11–15

That's Moses the Melancholic. Discouraged, depressed, wiped out. He had all of the symptoms of overload. All of his circuits popped at one time.

When you are in a state of overload, you have no desire to take action of any kind. Any little task is too much. You'll postpone making a phone call, running to the grocery store, and even fixing a meal. Overload leads to procrastination.

Pressure Myth.

Consider another reason for procrastination—one which is very subtle. Some people operate on the assumption that they work best under pressure. Therefore, they've developed a wait-to-the-last-minute life style for everything they do. Over the years they've trained themselves to get the adrenalin pumping as the deadline approaches. Because they complete the job in a short time, they feel terrific and confirm their assumption, *I work best under pressure.*

Many of us can work fairly well under pressure, because we are focusing our mental, emotional, and physical energies into a relatively short time period. Just as a magnifying glass focuses the sun's rays with such intensity that it burns paper, so can you focus your energy into such a small time frame that you light a fire under yourself and get the job done.

The questions you must address, however, are twofold. First, does this help you do your *best* work? And second, whose pressure are you under? I operate under pressure all the time, but the pressure is my own, imposed upon me by my deadlines. Therefore, when I feel that I'm going into overload, I'll back off and pace myself to a different beat of the drum.

Furthermore, planning well in advance, and working on parts of a project in advance, helps me pace myself at a rate in which I seldom feel overloaded. So you may work under pressure, but often the results are those of just getting by, rather than winning.

Self-Interest.

Self-interest also encourages many people to put off decisions and actions. The people of the United States cry out for a balanced budget year after year, but the self-interest of the politicians forces them to neglect the appropriate action and encourages them to continue applying Band-Aids to cancer patients.

Spiritualizing decision making.

Another interesting cause of procrastination among some Christians is to spiritualize their decisions. *When the Spirit moves me, I'll get started on that project. After I've prayed for several weeks, then I'll begin to work on that problem.* Or, *If God wants it to work out, He'll make it happen. He doesn't need me.*

The apostle James has an answer to those who put things off until they receive some magical signal from God. He writes, "Even so faith, if it has no works, is dead, being by itself" (James 2:17). The apostle Paul confirms the fact that God uses people to get things done and expects them to get involved, rather than to wait for some mystical experience. He says, " 'For whoever will call upon the name of the Lord will be saved.' How then shall they call upon Him in whom they have not believed? And how shall they believe in Him whom they have not heard? And how shall they hear without a preacher? And how shall they preach unless they are sent? . . ." (Rom. 10:13–15).

God uses people to preach. He also uses people to provide for the preachers to preach. The message which needs to get out to the world is urgent. It is not for some convenient time. It's a message of hope to a dying world. It's a cup of cold water to a man dying of thirst. Such decisions are not to be put off until tomorrow. The Spirit is leading, but not everyone is following.

The tyranny of the urgent.

A further common cause for putting off certain responsibilities is the urgent requests put upon us by friends, bosses, teachers, parents, children, and a host of others. The man who is burning the candle at both ends is wrapped up in the tyranny of the urgent. He needs sleep. He needs a diversion. He needs to pace himself. Instead, he just responds to all of the urgent pressures placed on him by sometimes well-meaning people. It's imperative not to become victimized by everyone else's urgent schedules.

Failure to distinguish between the essential and routine.

One other cause of procrastination is the failure to distinguish between what is essential and what is routine. Because we allow ourselves to get caught up in the routine responsibilities of life, we too often neglect what is really essential.

On one of His many travels, Jesus stopped by a well and sent His disciples to the next village for some supplies. While they were gone, a woman with an immoral reputation came out to the well for water. Jesus engaged the woman in conversation and soon revealed to her that He was the promised Messiah of Israel. When she understood who He was, she raced into the village and told the men that she had found the Messiah.

Meanwhile, the disciples returned to the well with their provisions and were ready to eat a tasty lunch. But Jesus did not have food on His mind. Instead, He looked toward the village, and seeing the multitudes rushing towards the well, He informed the disciples who were prepared to injest some delicious morsels: "Do you not say, 'There are yet four months, and then comes the harvest?' Behold, I say to you, lift up your eyes, and look in the fields, that they are white for harvest. Already he who reaps is receiving wages, and is gathering fruit for life eternal; that he who sows and he who reaps may rejoice together" (John 4:35–36).

The Lord wanted to draw their attention away from food (the routine) and focus it on the multitudes who were ready to hear the gospel (the essential).

Playing golf with your friends may be a routine for you, but spending that same time with your family could be essential. Reading the newspaper when you get home from work may be routine, but getting down on the floor and wrestling with your three-year-old could be essential. Buying another adult toy may be routine, but saving that money or giving that money to the Lord's work could be essential. As you learn to distinguish between the routine and the essential, you'll be less likely to put off doing those things which are really important in both value and results.

Now that you have had a glimpse of some reasons for procrastination, give your attention to the ways you can use for solving that problem which cripples your effectiveness in life.

How Can We Gain Victory over Procrastination?

Where should you begin to get a handle on the problem?

Define exactly what you must do.

Once you know where you're going, and the decision you must make, you've won half the battle. If you have a financial problem, your decision may be to begin working yourself out of debt, increasing your cash flow, or putting tight controls on your spending habits. If you are experiencing problems in your moral life, you may need to take action by breaking up with your boyfriend or girl friend, or committing yourself to a moral life style. If it's a marital problem, perhaps you should evaluate your own attitudes, seek a marriage counselor, or determine to see things from your spouse's viewpoint.

Before Joshua could take any action after the death of Moses, he needed to know exactly what he should do—otherwise, the nation of Israel might have stayed in the wilderness another forty years. The Book of Joshua states that after Moses died, God appeared to Joshua with a specific objective, "Moses My servant is dead; now therefore arise, cross this Jordan, you and all this people, to the land which I am giving to them, to the sons of Israel" (Josh. 1:2). Joshua knew where he should go and who he should take with him.

Visualize the benefits of completing your project.

Once you know what you must do, you'll need the appropriate motivation to carry you through the project. And one of the best motivators is to visualize the benefits of completing your project.

When I've decided to lose weight, I can usually stay motivated if I imagine what ten less pounds will feel like, or visualize my trousers fitting more loosely, or picture a flat stomach rather than a paunch.

The time I finally took the giant step to fix the drain in my sink, I was motivated by thinking how nice it would be to have water flowing freely down the drain with no messy cleanup afterward.

When God wanted Israel to take action on crossing into the Promised Land, He painted a magnificent landscape on the canvas of the people's imagination. He splashed that canvas with vivid color. He excited their taste buds with descriptive fruit. Moses expounded: "For the Lord your God is bringing you into a good land, a land of brooks of water, of fountains and springs, flowing forth in valleys and hills; a land of wheat and barley, of vines and fig trees and pomegranates, a land of olive oil and honey; a land where you shall eat food without scarcity, in which you shall not lack anything; a land whose stones are iron, and out of whose hills you can dig copper" (Deut. 8:7–9).

They could taste the figs, olives, and grapes. The land was so clear in their minds that they could smell the flowers. The people not only knew what to do, but now they were motivated to take action.

Visualize the negative consequences if action is neglected.

However, visualizing the positive results may not always be enough to motivate everyone. Sometimes we have to pause and consider the negative consequences of failing to take appropriate action. For instance, if you are experiencing a financial problem, but put off taking action, you may have a collection agency knocking at your door, or a nasty telephone call. Imagine yourself strangling on a dollar sign wrapped around your neck; or visualize yourself in a prison uniform with huge iron balls dragging at your feet, inscribed with the word DEBTS. Or you could visualize yourself saying good-bye to your neighbors, as they leave on their vacations, while you return to your house to sit and stare out the window in despair.

God made it quite clear what would happen if Israel failed to obey Him: "But it shall come about, if you will not obey the Lord your God, to observe to do all His commandments and His statutes which I charge you today, that all these curses shall come upon you and overtake you. . . . The Lord will send upon you curses, confusion, and rebuke, in all you undertake to do. . . . The Lord will make the pestilence cling to you. . . . The Lord will make the rain of your land powder and dust. . . . The Lord will cause you to be defeated before your enemies. . . ." (Deut. 28:15, 20, 21, 24–25).

If the blessing of taking action doesn't get you moving in the right direction, the curse from procrastinating may be just the motivation you need.

Set priorities.

Once you know what to do and can visualize both the positive and negative results of moving ahead or putting it off, you'll need to set some priorities.

When you set priorities, you are merely choosing one action over another. You are arranging the options in order of importance. Begin with the most important.

What is really essential?　You can choose to do a lot of things with your time, but what are the essentials in life? You may use up a lot of time, even energy, deciding whether to fly first class or coach. But if the plane begins to malfunction and spins toward the ground, seating assignments don't seem to matter a whole lot.

You may have heard the question about entering a dark room with a book of matches in your hand. For illustration sake, I want to repeat it. "What is the first thing you should do?" Most people would answer, "Light a match." That may sound like a good answer, but that action would be quite low on my priority list. The first thing I'd do is turn on the light switch, for it gives more light and saves the unnecessary activity of lighting a bunch of matches. Focus on the essential rather than the trivial. The next priority follows in logical sequence.

What will produce the best results?　There is a principle in finance known as "leverage," which means that we invest as little as possible with the hopes of gaining as much as possible. I believe there is another principle in existence which I call "reverse leverage." That's when we invest a ton of money and receive a dribble in return.

Many people expend massive amounts of energy with little or nothing to show for their efforts. They major in minors. They never pause long enough to ask, "Is the cost really worth it?" The Lord Himself encourages us to count the cost before taking action (Luke 14:28).

What will release the pressure? This is a third priority to consider. Too often this is the priority which the masses place higher on the list. You've heard it said, "The squeaky wheel gets the oil." Some people live as victims of everyone else's squeak. As soon as someone complains, the victim immediately goes into action to relieve the pressure. His life is thus spent accomplishing little, because he makes a habit of putting out someone else's fires. Keep pressure release lower on your list of priorities.

What do I enjoy doing? This is the priority that many individuals find most appealing. They refer to it as "doing my own thing." It's easy to procrastinate if we are using all or most of our time just doing those things which we most enjoy.

Joshua told the people that before they crossed over the Jordan River into the Promised Land, they needed to focus on a higher priority, "Then Joshua said to the people, 'Consecrate yourselves, for tomorrow the Lord will do wonders among you' " (Josh. 3:5). The people needed to get themselves right with God if they were to be His representatives in the Promised Land. They needed to set themselves apart from the peoples in the land and commit themselves to God alone. And that's an excellent priority to transfer into life today. Before I attempt anything for God, I'd better be committed to Him and be walking closely with Him.

Now you are ready for the actual step-by-step planning.

Plan your strategy.

Planning is nothing other than taking a large task and dividing it into many small tasks. So often we get overwhelmed when we look at large projects and responsibilities. *How will I ever get it finished? Where should I begin?* Planning reduces the overwhelming whole into manageable bite-sized units.

Once you reduce the whole into manageable tasks, you'll need to focus on one task at a time. When item 1 is completed, you can move on to item 2. Then set deadlines for each item you handle. Notice how Joshua operated under this principle.

The *whole* task was to enter the Promised Land. That was a gigantic responsibility. How could Joshua possibly move such a huge multitude from the wilderness to the Promised Land without mass confusion? Residents were living in that land then, as they do today. It was the original Palestinian problem. But note that Joshua reduces the major responsibility into manageable units:

(1) Send spies into the land (Josh. 2:1).
(2) Consecrate yourselves (3:5).
(3) Cross the Jordan (3:14).
(4) Priests enter the Jordan with the ark (3:15).
(5) Erect a memorial of stones (4:6–7).
(6) Priests come up out of Jordan (4:15–18).
(7) Circumcise the people (Josh. 5).
(8) Walk around Jericho and capture it on the seventh day (Josh. 6).

Now once you are organized and have your strategy planned, unless you take the first step toward your goal, your planning will have been in vain.

Take the first step.

Remember the train, as it prepared to pull out from the station? Even though it expended large amounts of energy, there was little to show for its initial efforts. But as the spinning wheels grabbed the rails, the train picked up speed and resumed its course towards the next city.

The first step in crossing the Jordan was taken by the priests. If they hadn't taken those first steps, the people could never have enjoyed the fruit of their labor. The story unfolds with the priests descending into the water:

> And when those who carried the ark came into the Jordan, and the feet of the priests carrying the ark were dipped in the edge of the water (for the Jordan overflows all its banks all the days of harvest), that the waters which were flowing down from above stood and rose up in one heap, a great distance away at Adam. . . . So the people crossed opposite Jericho. And the priests who carried the ark of the covenant of the Lord stood firm on dry ground in the middle of the Jordan while all Israel crossed on dry ground, until all the nation had finished crossing the Jordan.
>
> Joshua 3:15–17

Conclusion

Have you taken that first step? Do you have a plan by which you can get the job done? Do you know what to do first? Can you see the benefits of doing what you should or the consequences of continually putting off what you must do? Is it clear what action you must take?

Your life is made up of many options. Everyone is demanding a portion of your time. Everyone wants you to fit *their* schedule—but you can't please them all. You have to decide before God what is important. Then move ahead to resolve the issue.

In order to help you evaluate some possible areas in which you may be procrastinating, fill in the chart on the next page wherever it applies to you.

QUESTION	FINANCIAL LIFE	SPIRITUAL LIFE	FAMILY LIFE	PHYSICAL LIFE	MENTAL LIFE	SOCIAL LIFE
1. What have I been putting off?						
2. Why have I neglected to take action?						
3. What will be the benefits of moving forward on this project?						
4. What are the potential problems of neglecting this responsibility?						
5. When will I begin this task?						

PART II

MAKING TIME FOR YOURSELF

4

How Can You Know Where to Grow?

Introduction

One of the most obvious signs of life is growth. When life ceases, growth also discontinues. And so when growth is evident no longer, one might question how much real life still exists.

At the same time, not all areas of life experience the same degree of growth, for each area has a limited potential. For instance, the average female stops growing physically at about age eighteen, while the average male will reach his peak growth around age twenty-one.

\However, the potential for growing in our mental, social, spiritual, and personal relationships has no such limitation./ Most of us have not even tapped the potential for growth with which God has endowed us. How sad when people stop growing intellectually soon after they receive their high-school or college diploma. Even more tragic is when a young couple ceases to grow in love a few years after their honeymoon. But the clincher of them all is when Christians discontinue their spiritual growth soon after their new-birth experience. The writer to the Hebrews lamented:

For though by this time you ought to be teachers, you have need again for someone to teach you the elementary principles of the oracles of God, and you have come to need milk and not solid food. For everyone who partakes only of milk is not accustomed to the word of righteousness, for he is a babe. But solid food is for the mature, who because of practice have their senses trained to discern good and evil.

Hebrews 5:12–14

Growth was never meant to be optional, and yet many people treat it that way. Personal growth should not be looked upon as selfish or self-centered, for it is a natural result of life. However, it *can* be selfish and self-centered if one's growth has to come at the expense of others, such as the man who determines to grow in his career with no regard to his family; or the housewife who decides to launch a career without considering the impact it may have on the family. We see, then, that growth is essential for life and the natural result of life. However, when you consider all of the busyness of everyday activities and responsibilities, how can a person find the time to even consider growing? That's what this chapter will focus on. Through discernment, discovery, and discipline, you will be able to launch out into many meaningful growth areas of your life.

Discern an Area in Which You Would Like to Grow

If you were to ask the average person on the street to list the areas of life in which he'd like to grow, you'd probably receive a blank stare in response to your question. Much of the time we are not conscious of the needs, opportunities, or even those hidden interests that we might have for growing.

When Jesus spoke to the church at Laodicea, they were unaware of their spiritual condition. If a preacher had told them that they needed to change, they would have run him out of town. They felt secure and comfortable, but when the Lord spoke, the church perked up its ears:

I know your deeds, that you are neither cold nor hot; I would that you were cold or hot. So because you are lukewarm, and neither hot nor cold, I will spit you out of My mouth. Because

you say, "I am rich, and have become wealthy, and have need
of nothing," and you do not know that you are wretched and
miserable and poor and blind and naked. I advise you to buy
from Me gold refined by fire, that you may become rich, and
white garments, that you may clothe yourself, and that the shame
of your nakedness may not be revealed, and eyesalve to anoint
your eyes, that you may see.

Revelation 3:15–18

How then can our eyes be opened to our needs and opportunities? Here are several suggestions which may help you discern
areas for growth in your life.

Listen to others.

People have a way of pointing out both our strengths and
weaknesses. In the Old Testament Scriptures, when a man
needed to be rebuked or encouraged, God would send a
prophet. In David's case, the prophet Nathan had to rebuke
him and point out a need to change his moral and spiritual
life (2 Sam. 12). In the case of King Hezekiah, however, God
sent the prophet Isaiah to encourage him with the news of
fifteen additional years to his life (2 Kings 20).

Some people will be more than happy to point out your
shortcomings. Others will offer constructive criticism. And
then there are those few who will encourage you to pursue
some direction because of the potential they see in you. When
you are confronted by people, you have one of two choices
in how you can respond. You might respond defensively—or
as one who really wants to change what needs to be changed.
If you choose to be defensive, your growth will be limited
greatly. If you are open to suggestions, the sky is the limit
for growing. These messages may come from conversation,
reading books, listening to messages, or any number of ways.

See a need in your feelings of inadequacy.

We all have feelings of inadequacy. One man feels inadequate
because his occupation may not earn him the same amount

of money or carry the same prestige as that of a friend. One woman may feel inadequate because she fights a weight problem, while her close friend can eat what she wants and maintain the figure of a twenty-year-old coed. One student feels inferior to another who gets better grades.

These feelings of inadequacy may either discourage us from ever venturing forth to attempt something worthwhile, or they will spur us to turn those weaknesses into strengths, or to compensate in some other way—in other words, recognize our needs and do something about them.

Young Timothy felt inadequate because of his age. He needed an older, more mature and highly respected friend to remind him, "Let no one look down on your youthfulness, but rather in speech, conduct, love, faith, and purity, show yourself an example of those who believe" (1 Tim. 4:12). Paul encouraged him to grow in the areas of his strengths, and not excuse himself from effectiveness because he was young.

Look at your options.

Many times we don't even know where to start. When young people think about a future career, their ideas are usually very limited, because they don't know what's available. And adults aren't much better off.

For many years I had been aware that I was a slow reader, but I never thought that I would be able to do anything about it. After all, I had been through college and seminary, and had been in the ministry at the time for five years. If I couldn't read fast after all of that education, I never would. Or so I thought.

Then one day I heard an advertisement for a speed-reading seminar. Because of the great sense of need, the feeling of inadequacy, and now an opportunity to do something about my problem, I grabbed the chance, took the course, and never regretted it.

There are literally thousands of possible options for personal growth. An adult evening school, a city college or university catalog could help provoke thinking in possible areas to pursue. You might want to begin right in your own home and ask yourself, *How can I grow in my relationship with my spouse, my children, or my parents?* You may have some skills which could be finely honed.

Search the Scriptures.

Perhaps your greatest resource to point out needed areas for growth is the Bible itself. The Scriptures have a way of putting the finger on problem areas which could use improvement. In fact, the very purpose of the Word is to help a person grow towards maturity. Paul wrote, "All Scripture is inspired by God and *profitable* for teaching, for reproof, for correction, for training in righteousness; that the man of God may be *adequate, equipped* for every good work" (2 Tim. 3:16–17, *italics added*). He also wrote to the Colossians the reason he preached Christ, "And we proclaim Him, admonishing every man and teaching every man with all wisdom, that we may present every man *complete* in Christ" (Col. 1:28, *italics added*).

Learn from failure.

One other factor which helps you see where personal need exists is failure. When you've run up against a wall, and everything shatters around you, it's a good time to evaluate.

Have you ever plunged from a mountaintop experience into the valley of despair in a single day? A number of God's greatest have tasted the agony of defeat soon after the thrill of victory. Joshua is a case in point.

Israel's new leader had taken them to the walls of Jericho. With the blast of trumpets and a shout from the people, the walls tumbled, and Jericho became vulnerable to the invading Israeli army. However, between the victory of Joshua in chapter 6 and the defeat in chapter 7 lies a little word: *"But."* "But the sons of Israel acted unfaithfully . . ." (7:1).

Joshua, full of enthusiasm and able to taste another great victory, sent his troops into the town of Ai. But as his army confronted the enemy, Israel was defeated. The Bible describes the results, ". . . so the hearts of the people melted and became as water" (7:5). *Defeat.* No more drive—their courage drained from their veins. Israel saw only the black clouds of doom overhead. Hope had vanished.

What do you do when you're flat on your back? Give up? Quit? Turn inward? Joshua cried out to God in agony and asked for direction. He desperately needed to evaluate the problem and make changes.

Conclusion

If you've experienced failure in your marriage, your financial life, spiritual, or moral life, it's not the time to quit. It's imperative that you take time to evaluate the areas in which you need to grow. Discover what changes must be made and pursue that direction. Once you discern the area of need in your life, your next step is to discover ways in which you can grow.

5

How Can You Know How *to Grow?*

Introduction

In the last chapter, you discovered both the necessity for personal growth and the first step in personal growth. Since growth is a by-product of life itself, and because your own personal development pleases your Father in heaven, it is not an option. *God expects us to grow from the moment we come into the world to the very day we exit planet earth.*

You also learned that growth is not necessarily automatic. In fact, many individuals cease to grow in some very important areas of their lives, such as their marriage, their relationship with other people, their character, and often in their relationship with God.

One of the reasons they fail to grow is because it takes time and hard work. The path of least resistance is to coast through life and respond to life's problems and opportunities in an unwise and immature manner. Therefore, it is imperative to take the time to grow. Personal development will thus come through *discernment, discovery,* and *discipline.*

You've already seen how to discern areas in which you might want to grow, such as by responding properly to people who cross your path and who share observations with you, or by recognizing your needs through those feelings of inadequacy.

You've considered looking at the options for personal development and have considered the value of the Scriptures to point out areas of need in your personal life. Even failure can play a major role in helping you to understand where the growth needs to take place.

Once you decide on a specific area for growth, the next step is to discover ways in which you can grow—*how* to grow.

Discover Ways to Grow Personally

Though there are many situations and people that you would like to change, the only person you can really change is yourself. Therefore, personal growth is essential. How then do you begin a personal growth course?

Start with a clear observation.

Several years ago we used to play an observation game at our house. We would invite various people to the house and during the events of the evening, show them a painting of a Pennsylvania farm scene. We gave the participants about three minutes to study the painting. Then we had each one answer a series of twenty questions. One of those questions was, "Which direction was the plane flying, from left to right or right to left?" Most of the participants didn't recall even seeing a plane, but they took a guess anyway and wrote down the direction they thought it was traveling. Others did see a plane and were quite dogmatic about what they saw. Actually, there was no plane in the picture.

And that's the problem with our observation. We miss a lot of what actually exists and add to our perspective what never did exist. Whenever we observe anything and attempt to tell others what we have seen, we select only a fraction of what actually exists. Therefore, we need to use the available twenty-four hours of any given day to sharpen our focus and develop the ability to observe accurately. But what type of observations help one grow in his personal life?

Observe people.   One of the advantages of observation is that it doesn't demand a lot of extra time from your already-busy schedule. You can observe people as you work with them and talk with them. What has made their marriage so successful? Or why did they fail in their marriage? What could they do differently if they had it to do over?

The Scriptures often focus on the need to observe the lives of others. The writer to the Hebrews says, "Remember those who led you, who spoke the word of God to you; and considering the outcome of their way of life, *imitate their faith*" (Heb. 13:7, *italics added*). The apostle Paul also encouraged, "Be *imitators* of me, just as I also am of Christ" (1 Cor. 11:1, *italics added*).

The word translated "imitate" does not mean "to pretend" or "to mimic." Rather it means "to pattern after." A child often wants to be like dad. He sees certain qualities in his father which he appreciates. So he consciously or unconsciously patterns his life after his father.

As you observe people, you will see some character traits and methods of operation that will appeal to you, while others might repel you. Imitate what is good and helpful, but avoid what has hurt others.

Observe those who have lost money through a poor investment and avoid doing the same thing. However, observe the wise investor and grow in your financial life by following his example. Observe the individual who has developed good study habits, and learn from him. Avoid the undisciplined student who thinks that life owes him a living. Observe the disciplined person who sets goals in his physical, spiritual, and family life, and achieves those objectives. Then follow his example. But avoid following the example of that individual who is going nowhere with his life. Proverbs says it well, "He who walks with wise men will be wise, but the companion of fools will suffer harm" (Prov. 13:20).

Observe needs and opportunities. What needs exist which no one else seems to notice? Colonel Sanders saw a need to give people a good chicken dinner at a reasonable price. When he was in his seventies, he ventured into virgin territory and established his famous Kentucky Fried Chicken fast-food stores.

Ray Kroch, the fast-food entrepreneur, observed the line-up of people at a San Bernadino fast-food restaurant. Mr. Kroch sampled the french fries and was greatly impressed with the food, the service, and the management. He immediately envisioned similar restaurants all over the country—ones that would give people high quality food at a good price. At the age of fifty-two, when many men begin to think about retirement, Ray Kroch gave birth to one of the most successful restaurant businesses in the world: McDonald's.

You don't have to reinvent the mousetrap, but you might design a better one. There is always a better way to do what is already being done. You may want to write a better book, paint a better picture, or design a better building.

Moses grew in his ability to organize when he was willing to listen to advice from his father-in-law, Jethro (Exod. 18). Perhaps your growth potential is in leadership. Then learn to lead by observing effective leaders and seizing the opportunities which are available.

Develop in your personal life through experimentation.

Experimentation is an excellent teacher, but it is also a great threat to some. The individual who values security and is afraid to take risks will not like to experiment, but then neither will he grow in his personal life.

It would be wonderful if you had all of the answers to your questions before you ever sailed into uncharted waters, but life is full of probabilities, maybes, and ifs.

Think of Moses when he returned to Egypt after forty years of absence. His only security was God's faithfulness. He had no army, no plan of action, no backup of any kind if he failed. But Moses was willing to believe God, take the risk, and venture into enemy territory. Through this step of faith, Moses grew in his personal life into a man of great leadership.

There are two values with experimentation. It either can add a new direction to your life, or it may remove a possible direction from your life.

When my sons went to Mexico recently with our church youth on a missions project, it was a totally new experience. They were both hesitant to take the trip, but with some parental guidance, they took the step of faith. Both boys were challenged spiritually by the experience and for our older son, that experiment added a new direction to his life. Before the Mexico journey, Rick had considered medicine as his direction in life. After the trip, he pursued a new course—the ministry.

On the other hand, my younger son had considered the possibility of becoming a vet. So, to test the waters, he worked gratis for a local vet in his animal hospital. And though Steve thoroughly enjoyed his work, that experiment confirmed in his mind not to continue his course of veterinary medicine.

You may need to consider an area where you feel least secure and do some experimenting. For instance, if it is difficult for you to meet people because of being shy, why not put yourself in a situation where you *must* deal with the public? If you are a teenager, you might try a job where you deal with people over the counter or wait tables. If you're an adult, you might get involved with a ministry in the church in which you have to work closely with people. Experimentation and observation can take you a long way toward personal growth.

Grow through reading.

I realize that many people do not like to read. They feel that they never have the time, but reading is a must if you are going to develop your mental potential. Statistics reveal that out of the billions of cells in a person's brain, the average individual uses only 10 percent of his mind's capabilities during his entire lifetime. This means that from 10 to 11 billion brain cells remain unused at death.

Further statistics show that about 80 percent of the readers in our country are women. The majority of men, who usually claim that they are too busy to read, miss out on one of the greatest resources which can challenge them to grow. What should you read in order to stretch yourself and grow?

Read biographies. Learn from the experience of others. Why make the same mistakes that everyone else has been making? Why not read about the successes and failures of others? You could avoid duplicating their failures and transfer some of the means by which they've succeeded in life.

Biographies are helpful because you can often identify with the person—his fears and frustrations, his joys and expectations. And when biographies provide the added dimension of the Lord directing that life, you have the opportunity to grow spiritually.

This is why the Bible is such a fascinating book. It tells it "like it is." Scriptures don't cover up David's sin, or James's and John's selfish desire to put themselves at the head of the group, or Elijah's despair and Jonah's rebellion. At the same time, it shows how Paul turned from a persecutor to a preacher; how Peter changed from a denier to a dynamic disciple; and how Joseph the slave became Joseph the prime minister of Egypt.

Read idea-related books. There are books that challenge your thinking. They dislodge old attitudes which have clogged your thought processes over the years. Their authors are pacesetters who throw away the clichés and superficial problems of life; men and women who tell you what you need to hear, not what you want to hear. Such books are rare, but they must be read and responded to.

Idea-related books are often the voices of modern-day prophets who direct attention to the social, moral and spiritual problems of today. They speak about the Comfortable Pew; the Company of the Committed; the need for social action; discuss abortion; homosexuality; the care and feeding of the hungry; and the materialistic life style advocated and practiced by many evangelicals. They are the Elton Truebloods, the Francis Schaffers, the Tim LaHayes, and the Ron Siders. These modern-day prophets are like pieces of sand in an oyster. At first they agitate and produce discomfort, but eventually they become the catalyst for turning liabilities into valuable assets.

Read self-help books.   Another type of reading includes those books which add a practical flavor to life. They take ideas and put shoe leather on them. Such authors not only focus on what you should do and why you should do it, but also how to carry out the idea. There are books on how to read better and faster; how to discover your gifts; how to get control of your life; how to pray; how to witness; how to sell; how to type; how to manage your money wisely, and so forth.

Formal education basically prepares you to think. Unless your major in school falls into a skill area, you probably will be exposed to little practical information. I've personally discovered that seminary taught me the skill of how to study the Bible, but it fell far short of teaching how to pastor, to lead, to motivate others, or to administrate. All of that information had to be picked up through tapes, seminars, and reading self-help books.

Read inspirational books.   Sometimes you're not in the mood for new ideas. In fact, you don't want to strain your mind any longer on the problems of the world. You already know more about what needs to be done than what you are willing to do at this time. Therefore, you may be in need of inspirational reading. You need motivation to work toward a worthwhile goal. Such books may either be spiritually inspiring or emotionally inspiring.

Businessmen may get motivated as they read books by Zig Ziglar or Charlie Jones. Christians may get inspired spiritually when they read some of the classics by men like R. A. Torrey, Andrew Murray, or A. B. Simpson. Pastors may be challenged by the writings of other successful, dynamic pastors like Robert Schuller, W. A. Criswell or Dr. Donald Grey Barnhouse. Women will be encouraged as they read books by Joyce Landorf, Ann Kiemel Anderson and Jill Briscoe. Those who are handicapped will be blessed when they read the books of Joni Eareckson Tada. Those who have lost loved ones can be comforted when they read of the tragic experiences faced by Dale Evans Rogers or Joe Bayly.

One book which includes all of these types, plus many others, is the Bible itself.

Read the Bible. The Scriptures provide wisdom for your spiritual life, family life, moral life, financial life, emotional life, and all other areas in which you need to grow. The psalmist testifies: "O how I love Thy law! It is my meditation all the day. Thy commandments make me wiser than my enemies, for they are ever mine. I have more insight than all my teachers, for Thy testimonies are my meditation. I understand more than the aged, because I have observed Thy precepts" (Ps. 119:97–100).

Your teachers may know more about the subject they are teaching than you, but you may have greater wisdom about life than they do. The aged gain wisdom by years of experience, but a young person can develop tremendous amounts of wisdom as he assimilates biblical truth into his life.

Scripture provides moral wisdom—how to keep yourself pure, and why you should remain pure. It also offers great insight into management of your finances, including earning, spending, saving, investing, borrowing, and giving. It offers wisdom for family living. It tells you how to relate to other people; how to experience emotional stability; the value of life; the way of forgiveness; and how you can live better now and forever in eternity. The Bible opens an unlimited opportunity for personal growth.

So far you've seen the necessity of growing through observation, experimentation and reading. A fourth valuable ingredient is listening.

Grow through listening.

Listening is an art, and few of us have mastered it. Most people speak at 100 words per minute, but have the ability to listen at 400 words per minute. Perhaps our Creator is telling us that we should listen four times as much as we speak! In fact, one of the writers of Scripture bordered on that idea when he wrote, ". . . But let every one be *quick to hear, slow to speak* and slow to anger" (James 1:19, *italics added*).

Why is it, that after being introduced to someone, we haven't the foggiest notion what the person's name is? Poor listening. What therefore should we listen for?

Listen to what people say and don't say. One of the problems people have with listening is that their thoughts often focus more on their response to the conversation than on the conversation itself. For instance, if you receive a criticism, you may not really hear what is being said because your energies are diverted to defending your position. It would be better to ask, "How can I improve?" or, "Why is this person saying that?" rather than to angrily blast back, or run off whimpering like a whipped puppy.

You'll also want to listen to what is *not* said. Many people follow the theory, "If you can't say anything nice about a person, don't say anything at all."

Not long ago, I preached a different type of message than usual. It stretched me, and I'm glad I accepted the challenge. However, I was not very pleased with it. On the way home from church, my wife carried on a small talk conversation, without any reference to the morning message. After a few miles of this strained politeness, I looked over at her and queried, "Today's message apparently didn't rank as one of your all-time favorites, did it?" She laughed, and proceeded to share carefully how she really felt. I know now some of the changes I'd like to make in that message. This is part of my own growing experience in the area of preaching. If I want to be a better preacher, I need to be open to constructive criticism, even when it's not offered. Sometimes you just have to ask for it.

Listen to people's body language. One other aspect to listen for is how people speak to you with their body. They may tell you one thing with their words, but something entirely different with their shifting eyes, tight lips, red face, squirming gyrations, or slouching position.

Have you ever wondered why people don't understand or believe what you say at times? It could be your body language. Did you realize that people receive about 70 percent of the meaning of your message from your nonverbal language? In fact, children glean about 90 percent of the meaning from your body language. And when there is a conflict between what you say and the nonverbal communication, the nonverbal is accepted by the listener.

When a husband tells his wife with a deadpan expression and irritated tone, "I've already told you that I love you. What more do you want from me?" she is not hearing or experiencing love.

Therefore, when you carefully listen both to what is said as well as how it is being said, or even what is not being said, you'll learn about yourself, how people are relating to you, and the areas in which you need to grow.

If you've sung a solo in church; painted a picture; made a dress; built a cabinet for your stereo; or accomplished some other creative feat, and people respond by saying, "Oh, that's nice," you may consider going back to the drawing board.

But if they say, "Wow, that was terrific!" take it with a grain of salt and continue to develop in that area of your life.

Transform the problem into an opportunity.

A transformer changes an electric current from either a high to low potential (step-down transformer) or vice versa (step-up transformer), without changing the current energy. Likewise, when you are faced with a problem, you have a specific amount of energy to give to it. That energy can be used up by worrying about it, or it can be invested in transforming the problem into an opportunity.

The Bible indicates that God allows problems to enter our lives so that we grow through them. Paul writes:

> And not only this, but we also exult in our tribulations; knowing that tribulation brings about perseverance; and perseverance, proven character; and proven character, hope; and hope does not disappoint; because the love of God has been poured out within our hearts through the Holy Spirit who was given to us.
>
> Romans 5:3–5

Paul's imprisonment helped in reaching Caesar's household for Christ. John's exile to the island of Patmos provided him with the vision of the last days, which he recorded in the Book of Revelation. Joni Eareckson Tada's confinement to a wheelchair has enhanced her entire purpose for existence— she has been able to touch lives for Christ which would have never been changed had she not transformed her problem into an unprecedented opportunity. Robert H. Schuller illustrates this point in his book *Move Ahead with Possibility Thinking:*

> Norman Vincent Peale tells the story. He was stopped on the streets of New York by a man who said, "Reverend, I've got problems!" Dr. Peale answered, "Well, I know a place near here that has a population of fifteen thousand people and not a person has a problem." His troubled friend said, "Tell me, where is this place? I'd like to live there." And Dr. Peale answered, "It's Wood-lawn Cemetery in the Bronx!" Yes, it is only the dead who have

no problems. If you want to really live, you must dare to live adventurously. Every adventure creates its own particular and peculiar set of difficulties. You can protect yourself from problems by living a cautious life, but you may die of boredom (p. 67).

You may be facing a problem that seems insurmountable. You are wrestling with it daily, and it's getting the upper hand on you. Despair has set in. You begin to question God's purpose—maybe even His ability to handle the situation. Perhaps you've even wondered whether He exists any longer. That same amount of energy used to worry or to despair can also be used to make you strong and give you a renewed interest and purpose in life. Why not make it your growing edge? Make it work for you rather than against you. How is that done? By a renewed mind. A new perspective, through the power of God's Holy Spirit, "And do not be conformed to this world, but be transformed by the renewing of your mind . . ." (Rom. 12:2).

Where do you go from this point? You've discerned an area of need in your life. And you've discovered five ways to facilitate personal growth. However, the key to whether or not anything actually happens is your willingness to discipline yourself to make it happen.

Discipline Yourself to Grow

Discipline is merely learning to say *no* to one thing, so that you can say *yes* to something else. The problem we face is that we usually say no to the essentials of life, because we spend all of our time saying yes to many nonessentials. Here are four quick suggestions on how to get moving in the direction of personal growth through self-discipline.

Work the goal into your schedule.

Whatever you are determined to become in your growth area, work it into your schedule—no matter how busy you are. Put it closer to the top of your priority list.

At one time physical exercise was nothing but wishful thinking for me. Then I made a couple of hit-and-miss attempts to exercise, like once every three weeks or whenever the spirit moved, which was seldom. Finally, I realized that if I really wanted to develop an exercise program, it would have to become part of my routine week. I first had to cope with some immediate guilt feelings, because I felt that I should be working when I was exercising. Then I had to deal with everybody else's opinion—who also thought I should be working rather than exercising. Finally I made it part of my weekly routine.

When I was ministering in Winnipeg, I used to write out my messages. At that time, I followed this procedure for security reasons. Though I never preached from the written manuscripts, I felt more secure knowing that every word was available if I ever needed that information. When I moved to Fresno, however, I gave up the practice of writing out my sermons, because I had gained enough confidence to preach without a written manuscript as a backup. Also, I was able to save a minimum of five hours of preparation time each week.

However, there was one value I had neglected to realize by writing my message. This value is exposed in a quote from the great British poet, Francis Bacon, who wrote, "Reading maketh a *full* man, conference [speaking] maketh a *ready* man, and writing maketh an *exact* man" (*italics added*). That's what I felt was missing from my sermons—greater precision. I felt my preaching was getting sloppy, but I did not want to pay the price of an extra five hours each week to begin writing my messages again. Yet I knew that the only way to develop greater precision in sermon preparation would be to add another five hours to my schedule each week. And that is exactly what I have done over the past few months. Though this value may not show up as much in the delivery of my message, it has made a definite impact on the preparation of them.

Whatever goal you have established for yourself, take the necessary time to work it into your schedule. Make it part of your routine, whether it be physical exercise, a reading program, listening to cassette tapes, visiting people, or other such goals. *It must become part of your weekly schedule.*

Refuse to allow other pressures to interfere.

Of course, you must be flexible, but once you schedule your growth area into the week, allow only emergencies to cause you to deviate from your goal during those first few weeks. Once you allow the urgent matters to override your growth objective, the ball game is in the ninth inning. Another three strikes, and you're out.

I guarantee that as soon as you set specific goals for your personal growth, everyone and everything will do their best to interfere with those goals.

When I decide to go on a diet, everyone else wants me to join in fattening desserts. As soon as I determine to take more time for exercise, the work load increases tremendously. If I want to spend more time studying, the phone calls and problems mount in direct proportion.

You may decide that you will become a more effective father or mother by spending more time with your family. But don't be surprised when those nights that you set aside for the family will be bombarded by interruptions and opportunities to do something else.

Remember, the devil doesn't want you to grow. He wants you to remain immature. If he can keep you too busy to grow in your spiritual life or family relationships, you will become an easier target for him to shoot at. The lion usually attacks the straggler or the young. So does the devil prowl like a roaring lion, seeking whom he may devour.

Remind yourself why you want to grow in this area.

It's one thing to make a commitment to a specific goal, but it's another matter to follow through, especially when you run into resistance. In fact, before you decide to achieve in a particular area of life, you would be wise to list all of the reasons why it is important to you, as well as what changes you expect to see.

From a general perspective, a decision to grow personally is important for at least two excellent reasons.

Personal growth will increase your sense of self-worth. The average persons sells himself short of his potential. In fact, he uses a mere fraction of his real capability.

Jesus tells us to love our neighbors as ourselves. The reason many people don't love their neighbors is because they have a difficult time loving themselves. They live with a very low self-image. However, I know of few things that can increase a person's opinion of himself as much as a series of successful accomplishments.

A few years ago, my wife shared with me that she was beginning to wonder what contribution she was really making in people's lives. Her teaching had been on a maintenance level; our sons were becoming more independent; and my own ministry had really begun to blossom. She felt like the low one on the totem pole.

I encouraged her to pursue other possible opportunities in the school district in addition to teaching in the classroom. I also challenged her to go back to school and complete her master's degree. She accepted the challenge; applied for a new position with the school district; and succeeded in getting it. She also started her master's program at a local college. Within the first week of school, however, she suffered a back injury which required surgery. She was laid up for three months.

It seemed as if all of her dreams and goals would vanish with the injury, but instead of vanishing, those and other goals for personal development were realized.

During the past three years, Linda has been able to grow and expand her abilities in various areas. Because she excelled in her new position, she was offered another, more responsible position with the Fresno Unified School District. She has also been able to develop a daily, five-minute radio broadcast; complete her master's program; conduct speed-reading seminars; and travel throughout the country, speaking at retreats, churches, and seminars. I guarantee that today she feels much better about herself than she did a few short years ago.

Personal growth will give you a sense of purpose. Too many people with high potential keep it bottled up inside. They never discover what they can really do. They never answer the question, "Why am I here on earth, anyway?"

What unique contribution can you make to society? The fact that you lived so many years on earth means what? As you continue to tap that inner potential, you will experience a greater sense of purpose.

You may have the potential of being a tremendous prayer warrior who spends a lot of time interceding for others, who have a variety of hurts. You may have the potential of being a great musician, teacher, doctor, minister, businessman, or counselor.

Scientists tell us that there are huge amounts of untapped energy sources lying dormant, both under the earth and in the depths of the sea. I believe that there are even greater untapped resources in the lives of millions of people, who merely live from day to day with neither purpose nor a cutting edge to life.

Share your goal with a close friend for encouragement.

One final suggestion to help you discipline yourself is to share your plan of action with a friend for encouragement. When a friend knows what you are attempting to achieve, he can encourage you to continue during those difficult periods.

The writer of Proverbs wisely states, "Iron sharpens iron, so one man sharpens another" (Prov. 27:17). And Solomon adds, "Two are better than one, because they have a good return for their labor. For if either of them falls, the one will lift up his companion. But woe to the one who falls when there is not another to lift him up" (Eccl. 4:9–10).

The success of your personal growth progress may lie in the area of your support system. And that support personnel may be your spouse or another friend who is interested in your personal welfare.

Conclusion

Time is too short to waste in the routine of a given day. You have a vast reservoir of untapped energy and ability, which this world desperately needs. And you need to take the time to determine an area in which you should grow; discover specific ways by which you can grow; and discipline yourself to follow through on your commitment to growth.

PART III

MAKING TIME FOR YOUR FAMILY

6

Dad, Evaluate Your Investment

Introduction

Investments today are risky at best. You could lose your life savings; tie up cash indefinitely; or, if lucky, make a few dollars. But there is one investment that guarantees a very profitable return. It's a long-term investment program, with dividends compounding every year, and promising generous payments for the rest of your life.

That investment program is expressed in several Proverbs (*italics are added*): "Train up a child in the way he should go, even when *he is old he will not depart from it*" (22:6); "The rod and reproof *give wisdom,* but a child who gets his own way brings shame to his mother" (29:15); "Correct your son, and *he will give you comfort; he will also delight your soul*" (29:17).

Just as you make investments with the hope of providing some financial security for your later years, so you need to make time investments in your children if you are seeking a solid and secure relationship with them in later life. The Bible says, "Do not be deceived, God is not mocked; for whatever a man sows, this he will also reap" (Gal. 6:7). Again it says, "Now this I say, he who sows sparingly shall also reap sparingly; and he who sows bountifully shall also reap bountifully" (2 Cor. 9:6).

You reap in kind as you sow. Invest little time in your children now, and in later life, they will invest little time in you. Make time to build solid relationships with your children when they are young, and they will make time to sustain that relationship when they mature.

But how will investing time in your children's lives build a solid relationship for the future? You read a lot about drugs and sexual promiscuity among teenagers. Many young people are rebelling against their parents' value system. Traditional attitudes, values, and priorities hold little interest among a significant segment of the American teenage population. What has gone wrong?

Certainly many factors are involved in the decline of formerly held values, but the failure of parents to invest quality time in their children has to place near the top of the list.

Yet if someone were to ask you how much time you really spend with your children, you would probably give yourself an overrated evaluation. In her book *Tough and Tender,* Joyce Landorf informs her readers, "In a recent study by Cornell University, 200 fathers were asked to estimate how much time they spent daily with each of their children. The men estimated they spent an average of fifteen minutes per day per child. Then the children were fitted with tape-recording devices, and the actual time was clocked. The final studies showed that the average time each man actually spent with a child per day was thirty-seven seconds!" (p. 89).

That's tragic. But even if these fathers had actually spent fifteen minutes, the prospects of developing strong, lasting relationships would be dim. Time is essential for a child to sense dad's love and to develop a healthy self-image. Time is also required for fathers to provide a healthy model which the child can follow, and to allow Dad to really know and understand his child. Let's look at several ways in which your time investment will build a solid relationship between you and your child. (Although this chapter is primarily directed to fathers, there is much here for mothers too.)

Invest Your Time to Build a Solid Relationship between You and Your Child

Your investment of time will communicate love to your child.

Most fathers take the role of "provider" seriously. They feel responsible for the physical well-being of their family, so they work long hours to meet the needs and comforts of life. However, a child's security is not so much in what dad provides materially, as it is in what he gives *of himself.* In my own home, we never had an abundance of material advantage over other kids. In fact, I was thirteen years old before our family owned its first car, but none of us ever felt deprived. Our family has always had a close relationship with one another. We knew that we were loved.

Tim LaHaye speaks of a judge in juvenile court in his book *Spirit-Controlled Family Living.* He says, "A juvenile-court judge, after presiding over thousands of juvenile cases, observed, 'I have yet to see a boy come before my court who had a father who took him fishing or went to ball games or spent time with him.'" LaHaye then concludes, "It has been my observation that the father who demonstrates his love for his children by making time for teaching them, no matter how busy his schedule, enjoys his children when they are adults" (p. 140).

Your investment of time builds your child's self-esteem.

The investment of time not only tells your child, "I love you," but also builds a good self-image. The Bible says, "For as he thinks within himself, so he is . . ." (Prov. 23:7). If a child thinks he is unloved or unworthy, it will show up in his attitudes and behavior. Likewise, if his self-esteem is positive, he will be able to think well of others and relate to them in a proper way. The self-image is developed primarily in the home.

Dr. James Dobson writes in *Hide or Seek,* "A sizable portion of your child's self-concept emerges from the way he thinks you 'see' him." Dobson continues. . . .

It takes time to be an effective parent when children are small. It takes time to introduce them to good books—it takes time to fly kites and play punch ball and put together jigsaw puzzles. It takes time to listen, once more, to the skinned-knee episode and talk about the bird with the broken wing. These are the building blocks of esteem, held together with the mortar of love. But they seldom materialize amidst busy timetables. Instead, crowded lives produce fatigue—and fatigue produces irritability—and irritability produces indifference—and indifference can be interpreted by the child as a lack of genuine affection and personal esteem.

Your investment of time provides a model for your child.

Another way in which time with your child builds a solid base for future relationships is by offering the opportunity to establish a model which your child can follow. Children are continually looking for models after which they can pattern their lives. They want to be like someone, and dad can become that positive model if he is available. However, the child whose dad is absent will have to look elsewhere. He may search for his models among sports figures, rock stars, or TV personalities. In fact, most children spend more time with television than with either of their parents. According to Nielsen ratings recently, an average American household watched 6½ hours of TV a day, 7½ if on cable. Preschool children spent 29 hours a week Children aged 6–11 watched almost 26 hours a week (*Dad's Only,* October 1981). When you consider what type of models TV offers on how to be a man, a father, or a husband, you can imagine what your child is learning.

Your time investment helps you to understand your child in greater depth.

A fourth way in which time investment can help you build a solid relationship for the future is by giving you opportunity to understand your child in greater depth. It's easy for a father (or mother) to become preoccupied with work and activity. As his time is consumed outside the family, however, he misses many choice opportunities to really know his child. True, he may remember a birthday, or know that his son hates broccoli, and his daughter despises cleaning her room, but he really doesn't *know* his child intimately—how he feels, thinks, his potential, his problem areas, or even his friends.

What is your child thinking? Do you have any idea what fills the mind of your child? What about those questions he wrestles with? Are you familiar with his plans, ambitions, and dreams?

The Bible says, "A plan in the heart of a man is like deep water, but a man of understanding draws it out" (Prov. 20:5). Your child may have a vague understanding of what he or she wants to do or would like to become, but your child needs you to probe, to encourage, and to challenge, so that these vague ideas crystalize and focus on what will help maximize his or her potential.

When my older son was planning to enter college, during the years before he graduated from high school, we visited various campuses, looked at catalogs, and talked with administrators and professors. Since he was seven years of age, Rick had talked about medicine. Therefore, the schools we visited provided excellent premed programs. After comparing colleges, my son narrowed his choice to two campuses, and then made his decision. We thought his choice was wise on the basis of the assumptions he used to make that decision.

However, recently he began talking again about the school he was planning to attend. As we continued the conversation, some yellow flags emerged. Finally I raised a question which challenged the assumption of his wanting to be a doctor. In response, Rick said, "Dad, I don't really think I want to go into medicine. For quite a while now, I've considered another direction. And in the last few days, it's becoming clearer to me that I should seriously think about going into the ministry."

I have to admit that I was somewhat taken aback, but certainly not disappointed. I said, "Son, let's just say that you've closed the doors on medicine and are looking at the possibility of ministry. There are other options which you may not be aware of at this point in your life. I'm thrilled that ministry is high on your priority list. Keep in mind, it's one area which you want to be certain before you commit yourself to it."

Once the assumptions changed, the direction and the schools changed. Today Rick is pursuing a career in the ministry. Time will tell whether he continues that direction, but as I look back on our encounter, I am thankful that I was at the right place at the right time to draw out of him those questions and desires which he had never verbalized.

What is your child feeling? Not only are thoughts often hidden from parents, but feelings are also camouflaged. Some children wear their feelings on their shirt sleeves, while others keep them hidden deep within the recesses of their hearts. Your child may be feeling fear, inadequacy, guilt, frustration, anger, hostility, peace, anxiety, and so forth. If poor communication exists between parent and child, those feelings will remain hidden for a period of time. Then one day an explosion may rock the house, as the child vents his feelings. So, parents, prevent the problem by discovering your child's feelings.

What are your child's strengths and weaknesses? Another aspect of a child's life which demands clear understanding is his strengths and weaknesses. The Scriptures provide a beautiful model of a father-child relationship on a spiritual rather than physical level. That model is Paul and Timothy. The apostle often refers to Timothy as his son, and related to Timothy as he would a physical son. And Timothy responded in like manner.

In his Epistle to the Philippians, the apostle writes:

> But I hope in the Lord Jesus to send Timothy to you shortly, so that I also may be encouraged when I learn of your condition. For I have no one else of kindred spirit who will genuinely be

concerned for your welfare. For they all seek after their own interests, not those of Christ Jesus. But you know of his proven worth that he served with me in the furtherance of the gospel like a child serving his father.

Philippians 2:19–22

Paul knew Timothy's strengths. He was a young man who had genuine interest in other people. He was also faithful, committed to the needs of others.

But Timothy also had some specific weaknesses which needed to be transformed into strengths. So Paul wrote two personal letters to his young son in the faith and encouraged Timothy to strengthen those weak points. "Let no one look down on your youthfulness, but rather in speech, conduct, love, faith and purity, show yourself an example of those who believe. . . . Do not neglect the spiritual gift within you . . ." (1 Tim. 4:12, 14). "For this reason I remind you to kindle afresh the gift of God which is in you through the laying on of my hands. For God has not given us a spirit of timidity, but of power and love and discipline" (2 Tim. 1:6–7). Timothy had a timid streak in him. In spite of his potential, he was using only a small portion of it. Since Paul had spent adequate time getting to know Timothy, he was able to encourage him to develop his gift and become the person God designed him to be.

Dad, you can only encourage your child to discover what you've already discovered in him and to develop the resources which God has given to him.

Who are your child's friends? There is another major part of your child's life demanding your understanding. That is to know and to relate well to his friends. How well do you know and relate to the kids whom your son or daughter has chosen for his (her) peer group?

In some households, the children are never allowed to bring their friends into the house. In other homes, the friends come and go, but seldom does dad take the time to know them.

The psalmist declared, "I am a companion of all those who

fear Thee, and of those who keep Thy precepts" (Ps. 119:63). In Proverbs it's stated, "He who walks with wise men will be wise, but the companion of fools will suffer harm" (13:20).

Do you know your child's friends? What about their values? Tastes? Ambitions? Moral standards? Trustworthiness? Habits? Your child will be influenced greatly by the pressure they exert on him.

My wife and I have made it a point since our children were young to open our house as the meeting center for their friends. Our house has always been filled with children and young people, because we wanted to know with whom our boys spent time. We also wanted to have a positive influence on those friends.

A father's time investment in his children will help pave the way for a solid relationship in the future by communicating his love to the child; building his child's self-esteem; providing a model for the child to follow; and helping dad to understand his child.

But where should you go from there? What objectives should you focus on when you are with your child?

You Should Focus on Five Basic Objectives, When You Invest Time with Your Child

Give your child the opportunity to know you intimately.

Sometimes dads don't realize in how much high esteem their children hold them. For some kids, "Dad can do no wrong." Remember those arguments you'd get into when you were a little kid? "My dad can beat up your dad." "My dad is smarter than your dad." When I was young, I thought that my dad was the smartest person in the world. He was an engineer, so I assumed that he was brilliant in math. And that was a hard act to follow, because math was not my favorite subject. However, I'll never forget one night, as I was having difficulty with a math problem, I threw down my pencil and complained to my dad, "I'll never understand this." As he unsuccessfully attempted to encourage me, I retorted, "How would you know what it's like? Math was always easy for you." To my surprise, dad replied, "That's not true. Math was not easy for me. Many times it was a struggle, but I worked hard at it and eventually learned to enjoy it." Wow! What a revelation! My dad wasn't perfect. He had struggles just as I did. Maybe there was hope for me also.

I've never forgotten that point of vulnerability, when dad was willing to share some of his struggles with me. So I've carried on the tradition. Today my sons have no illusions about my brilliance. They've heard and witnessed some of my struggles. I've shared the times of difficult decisions. They've heard about my failures, as well as my successes. And though I've always encouraged them to strive for excellence in whatever they attempt, I never demand perfection. I may challenge them to reach beyond their performance, but not beyond their potential.

Communicate your love and support for your child.

Another opportunity before you is to communicate your love and support for your child.

I have no doubts that you love your children—and *you* know how much you love them. But do *they* understand your love for them? Are you communicating your love on a level that they feel loved and supported by you?

A National Gallup Youth Survey taken among one-thousand teenagers in 1981 reveals that 25 percent do not discuss their day's activities with their parents. Forty-two percent said they had not received parental words of praise during the twenty-four-hour period tested. Half had not gotten a hug or kiss, and 54 percent had not heard the words "I love you." Seventy-nine percent said they had not been helped with homework by a parent (*Dad's Only,* March 1981).

A pastor friend of mine, who is serving in a small church

at present, has had several opportunities to move to larger and more prestigious churches. He rejected the offers for one very basic reason. He told me, "We live in a great area for rearing children. It's an excellent environment, and my children have developed a lot of friends. For their sake, I've said no. However, if I were convinced that God was moving me to another church, I'd be ready to go." You may not agree entirely with his reasoning, but that is the judgment call he made, with great peace in his decision. Though his children may not be old enough to appreciate his sacrifice, they will benefit from that decision.

You should model a godly life style before your children.

Dad, you are a model for your child. He wants to be just like you. The question each of us needs to ask ourselves is, "What am I modeling for my child?"

David set an example of moral impurity for his son Amnon. As David was unfaithful by taking Bathsheba unto himself, so his son Amnon sinned against his half-sister, Tamar, and defiled her virginity (2 Sam. 13:14).

In contrast, the apostle Paul provided an excellent example for Timothy. He wrote, "But you followed my teaching, conduct, purpose, faith, patience, love, perseverance, persecutions, sufferings . . ." (2 Tim. 3:10–11).

In his book *Confident Children and How They Grow,* Dr. Richard Strauss writes:

> A boy particularly needs to know his dad. Dad represents the man he will become—the husband he will be to his wife, the father he will be to his children, the provider he will be for his family, the leader he will be in his church, and the witness he will be in the world. He needs an example to follow, a model to identify with, a dad he can be proud of—sons tend to repeat the pattern set by their fathers in marriage . . . Dad, spend time with your boy (pp. 125–26).

And what about daughters? Do they emulate their dads? Strauss continues:

> Daughters, too, need to know their dads. A girl learns from her dad what men are like. He represents the husband she will one day give herself to, the father of her children, the authority figure she will submit to. It has been observed that a girl often subconsciously seeks a husband like her father. So, become the kind of husband you want your daughter to marry. Then cultivate a warm and cordial relationship with her (p. 126).

My grandfather was known as a man of integrity. My dad has the reputation of a man who has much integrity. Therefore, I've asked God to help me become a man of integrity because this is what I want for my sons. My greatest desire for my sons, above anything else they may achieve in life, was penned by the apostle John in his later years. He wrote, "I have no greater joy than this, to hear of my children walking in the truth" (3 John 4). As I walk in the truth, they will be able to observe how truth can motivate, guide, and free a man to become what God designed him to be. Truth in one's life doesn't have to be strait-laced and sober-faced. It can be fun, exhilarating and fulfilling.

Teach your child biblical values.

What else can you do with the time you invest in your children? Teach them a value system which will not change with the latest fad. Young children need to know the value of friendship, money, character, giving of oneself, investing in the lives of others, a personal relationship with God, moral purity, hard work, honesty, responsible freedom, and other such values.

The Book of Proverbs is filled with values, which a father was communicating to his son, "My son, do not forget my teaching. . . ." "My son, do not reject the discipline of the Lord; or loathe His reproof. . . ." "Listen to your father who

begot you, and do not despise your mother when she is old."
"Give me your heart, my son, and let your eyes delight in
my ways. For a harlot is a deep pit, and an adulterous woman
is a narrow well" (3:1, 11; 23:22, 26–27).

Children who discard their parents' values later in life do
not neglect them because the values are deficient. Instead, they
cast the values aside, because they never really worked for
their parents. As Paul aptly expressed it, "You, therefore, who
teach another, do you not teach yourself? You who preach
that one should not steal, do you steal? You who say that
one should not commit adultery, do you commit adultery?
You who abhor idols, do you rob temples? You who boast
in the Law, through your breaking the Law, do you dishonor
God?" (Rom. 2:21–23).

Discipline your child.

Along with teaching your children biblical values, comes
the responsibility of disciplining them. The Old Testament describes a sad family relationship between a Jewish priest and
his two sons. Actually the only relationship they seemed to
have was that the same blood flowed through their veins. Perhaps Eli was so busy doing the Lord's work that he neglected
to invest prime time in his children. Listen to the tragic descrip-
tion of these two sons when they became young adults:

Now the sons of Eli were worthless men; they did not know the
Lord and the custom of the priests with the people. . . . Now
Eli was very old; and he heard all that his sons were doing to
all Israel, and how they lay with the women who served at the
doorway of the tent of meeting. And he said to them, "Why do
you do such things, the evil things that I hear from all these
people? No, my sons; for the report is not good which I hear
the Lord's people circulating. If one man sins against another,
God will mediate for him; but if a man sins against the Lord,
who can intercede for him?" *But they would not listen* to the
voice of their father, for the Lord desired to put them to death.
1 Samuel 2:12–13, 22–25, (*italics added*)

Why would they not listen to their father? Fundamentally, because the rebuke was too little, too late. Eli waited until their behavioral patterns had already been solidly set in concrete. Because of this neglect, God had to rebuke Eli by sending a message to him through Samuel. The message declared, "In that day I will carry out against Eli all that I have spoken concerning his house, from beginning to end. For I have told him that I am about to judge his house forever for the iniquity which he knew, because his sons brought a curse on themselves and he did not rebuke them" (1 Sam. 3:12–13).

Children need to be disciplined for their own good. The Bible reveals that a father who refuses to discipline his child does not really love his child (Heb. 12:5–8).

The purpose of discipline is not so that fathers can vent their anger. Discipline has a fourfold purpose, according to the Book of Hebrews: (1) to communicate dad's love to his child (12:5–8); (2) to teach the child respect for all authority (12:9); (3) to develop godly character in the child's life (Heb. 12:10); and (4) to help the child enjoy a life of personal peace (12:11).

You are now aware of the importance of investing time in your child, and the objectives to accomplish when you are with him. The major problem now confronting you is how to find the time to invest in your child's life.

Apply These Methods, As You Invest Time in Your Child

There are hundreds of ways to invest time with your children, but here are five well-tried and -tested methods of making your time investment work wonders.

Turn your desire into a goal.

Earlier in this book I mentioned the importance of setting goals which are specific and measurable. Well, most dads just dream about more time with the family. You need to change from dreaming ("I'd like to spend more time with my kids"), to action ("I will set aside Monday and Thursday evenings, plus all day Saturday for my children").

In his excellent book, *When I Relax I Feel Guilty,* Tim Hansel shares a poem written especially for us busy dads who get caught up in the hustle and bustle of life. It's entitled "Slow Me Down, Lord."

Slow Me Down, Lord

Slow me down, Lord.
Ease the pounding of my heart by the quieting of my mind.
Steady my hurried pace with a vision of the eternal reach of time.
Give me, amid the confusion of the day, the calmness of the everlasting hills.
Break the tensions of my nerves and muscles with the soothing music of the singing streams that live in my memory.
Teach me the art of taking minute vacations—of slowing down to look at a flower, to chat with a friend, to pat a dog, to smile at a child, to read a few lines from a good book.
Slow me down, Lord, and inspire me to send my roots deep into the soil of life's enduring values, that I may grow toward my greater destiny.
Remind me each day that the race is not always to the swift; that there is more to life than increasing its speed.
Let me look upward to the towering oak and know that it grew great and strong because it grew slowly and well.

Orin L. Crain

Use those natural times with your child to greatest advantage.

For instance, what do you do at mealtimes? Do you talk? Listen? Laugh? Evaluate the day? or just eat and run? Mealtimes offer tremendous opportunities to get on the wavelength of your children's lives.

Early evening offers great opportunities to play games, wres-

tle on the floor, play outside, build things, or work together
on various projects. When our boys were small, we would
go for walks or play football outside. Sometimes we'd just
hop in the car and go for a drive or go to an ice-cream store
for a snack.

And then there are those priceless moments at bedtime.
It's a time of reflection. A time to pray together. A time for
your children to share the fun they had that day, or maybe
vent some of their anxieties about tomorrow. These are built-
in times which need to be used to their ultimate potential.

Involve yourself in your child's interests and activities.

It might be Little League, soccer, or football. You might
be able to coach, assist, or just attend as a supporter for your
child. Your child's interest may be in the school band or orchestra. He may get involved in the drama department or in debat-
ing or the 4-H Club.

Dad, when your son or daughter is performing, you need
to be there, if at all possible. Even a phone call or letter would
help, if you are out of town at that time. Perhaps you could
let your child know that you will be praying for him, as he
is taking his major test today. You may involve yourself in
his interests by driving him to his piano lessons, teaching him
to fish, or showing him how to build model airplanes.

My dad's work took him out of town often as I was growing
up. When he was in town, however, I vividly remember his
attending those orchestra concerts, swimming meets, and gym-
nastics events in which I participated. I was so proud and
grateful that he cared enough to come.

Develop a hobby with your child.

Another way to invest your time is to interest your child
in a hobby. I used to develop my own black and white film.
Although our sons were only four and five years old, I would

take them into the darkroom and let them move the film from one pan to another, and watch their faces light up, as they observed an image appear on the white photographic paper. The boys later developed an interest of their own in making movies. They went so far as to write scripts, shoot action scenes, which included people falling into swimming pools, off roofs, and out of trees. They created their own movie company, "Yohnson Productions," named after the two families involved, the Yohns and the Andersons.

Today our younger son is involved with video taping special services at church, including musical presentations and weddings. What was once my hobby has today become the hobby of my sons.

Work with him around the house.

Another use of your time with your child could include working around the house. One of the goals that my wife and I have had for our children was that they become self-sufficient. We wanted them to be able to cook their own meals, shop for groceries, clean the house, keep the lawn trimmed, wash and iron their clothes, manage money, and other such responsibilities. Therefore, each boy was given specific tasks, and though some of those assignments are handled alone, others can be fulfilled as a team. Working with your child not only conveys the value of hard work, but also offers opportunity to talk. Many times my sons and I have been able to talk, as we pulled weeds together or worked on a broken lawn sprinkler.

Conclusion

Is your time investment going to be worth it? If you pay the price to give up some things you might enjoy for yourself just to spend time with your children, will it pay generous dividends in the future?

Back in 1974, Sandy and Harry Chapin wrote a song which vividly describes what happens when dads neglect to invest time in their children. Listen to it sometime and then answer this question for yourself—will my time investment in my children be worth the price I have to pay?

The song, "Cat's in the Cradle," tells the all-too-familiar story of a father too busy to spend time with his growing son. The boy loves his father, even though he is rarely with him, and vows that he is going to be "just like you, Dad." Soon the little boy is in college and too busy for his father. The son marries, has his own family, and becomes busier than ever. Now it is the father asking when they can "get together." The roles are reversed, and it occurs to the father that, indeed, his son did become *just like him.*

What kind of future relationship do you want with your children? If you want a close and abiding relationship, it's going to cost you something—your time.

7

Effective Mothering Takes Time

Introduction

We live in a busy world. Not only does work expand to fill the time available, but interests and demands expand as well. A generation ago, mothers understood their role and responsibilities quite well. They remained in the home, kept house, and cared for the children. These responsibilities in themselves kept most women very busy.

Today the domestic scene has changed. According to *Newsweek* (19 May 1980) 43 percent of all mothers with children ages from infancy to six are now in the work force. Sixty-four percent of all children between the ages of three and five spend part of their day in facilities outside of the home. So much of the time which was invested at home in the lives of young children is now spent in the work force.

There are time demands other than that of the work force. Some mothers are investing their time in advancing their education, often during those formative years of their children. Volunteer organizations and civic responsibilities also drain away time and energy from mothers who could be devoting it to their children.

In her book *How Do You Find the Time*, Pat King asks:

How does a Christian mother find enough time . . . ? The basic fact is this: children take time. Therein lies the misery. There is so much we want to do, so much needing to be done in this world of ours, so much that society insists that we must do. We must not have ring around the collar, we must have floors that gleam until we can see our faces in them, we must have furniture that reflects an arranged bouquet in living color. We must cook gourmet meals, be publicly aware, socially active, academically current. Then, of course, we have the children to take care of, and the children take so much time.

Training up a child takes time . . . discipline takes both time and energy, and instruction in the Lord must go on and on. As we add training, disciplining and instructing to the list of feeding, cleaning, teaching, listening, and supporting, it's easy to see why we may be miserable. All these things that must be done with our children are at war with all that society tells us, or that we tell ourselves, we must do elsewhere (*Getting More Done in Less Time, and Having More Fun Doing It,* p. 74).

How can a woman be an effective mother in the midst of these time pressures and responsibilities? How can a mother find time to care for her children and establish a personal life for herself as well? There is no secret formula or magic key which will unlock vast amounts of extra time. However, there are some proven principles which can help a busy mother also become an effective mother. Let's begin with the principle of avoiding child-rearing mythology.

Don't Buy into the Prevailing Child-Rearing Myths

Today's marketplace is filled with many prevalent child-rearing myths, which authors and lecturers peddle to unsuspecting young mothers. Many women unknowingly buy into child-rearing principles, which have absolutely no foundation or support. Consider, for instance, this prevalent myth.

Children will automatically accept and live by their parents' beliefs and values.

Some parents see no need to invest much time in their children, because they believe that as long as they themselves are good people, their children will conform to their standards.

Such parents take their children to church, supposing that with a church background, plus a fairly nice home background, the children will grow up loving God and other people. However, both Scripture and experience demonstrate the fallacy of this position.

Biblical evidence denies this perspective. In the last chapter, I referred to Eli, who was a priest of Israel, during the time when the Judges ruled that nation. Eli himself was a godly man—a man of the cloth—but what about his sons? You recall that their conduct is recorded in Holy Scripture: "Now the sons of Eli were worthless men; they did not know the Lord and the custom of the priests with the people . . ." (1 Sam. 2:12–13).

The Scripture goes on to tell us just how thoroughly worthless Eli's sons were. Eventually news of their transgressions got back to their father, who tried to warn them—too little and too late! The sons were killed by the Philistines, for the Lord desired that they die. This example illustrates that good parents don't necessarily produce good children. In addition to this biblical evidence, there is also historical evidence that children will not automatically accept and live by their parents' beliefs and values.

Historical evidence denies this perspective. If history shows us anything, it demonstrates that one generation does not necessarily follow in the footsteps of the previous generation. In fact, often through history there has been a swing of the pendulum. Think of the changes that have taken place in the past thirty years in the United States.

In the 1950s there was no rating system for movies. There was no need for one. Most of what was shown on the screen could be viewed by the average family without offense. Today, however, it can be an embarrassment for families, as they watch television.

The sexual revolution has been sweeping this country for the past two decades. In recent years, an epidemic of venereal disease has spread out of control, including new, often-fatal strains. At the same time, solutions being proposed to deal with the problem are merely dealing with the symptoms. The solution to the problem of venereal disease is moral purity, but no one seems to want to pay such a high price to solve this devastating problem.

No, children do not automatically accept and live by their parents' beliefs and values. Beliefs and values can change from one generation to the next, unless parents are willing to spend the time to transmit those beliefs and values to their children. Consider still another myth.

Children are most greatly influenced by their home life.

It is true that 85 percent of a child's personality is formed by the time he reaches age six. It is also true that a child spends 83 percent of his time in the home. But there are other strong influences on the child, which shape his personality, character, attitudes, and behavior.

Television. The present generation of children is quite different from their parents in the number of hours they watch TV. According to Dr. Gerald Looney, University of Arizona, "By the time the average pre-school child reaches fourteen years of age, he will have witnessed 18,000 murders on television, and countless hours of related violence, nonsense and unadulterated dribble!" Furthermore, Dr. Saul Kapel states, "The most time consuming activity in the life of a child is neither school nor family interaction. It is television, absorbing 14,000 valuable hours during the course of childhood! That is equivalent to sitting before the tube eight hours a day, continuously for 4.9 years!" (*Dr. Dobson Answers Your Questions*, p. 457). In addition to television, consider the influence that school has on the child.

School. Not only is a child influenced by the subjects he learns at school, but he is also greatly influenced by the teachers who instruct him. Many of the values and life styles of teachers today do not reflect a biblical value system. The language some teachers use; their viewpoint of sexual freedom; or their sometimes excessive use of alcoholic beverages—as well as their competition with one another to climb to the top of the ladder—will model for students a life style that really excludes God. Along with the influence of school, is the pressure which peers bring to bear on the child.

Peer-group pressure. When your child reaches the teen years, other voices beckon to him and challenge his values and beliefs which he has learned in the home. Those voices come from individuals with whom he can closely identify. This happens at the stage of his life when he is growing away from parental authority and developing his own independence. He begins to march to the beat of a different drummer.

Personal desires and interest are added to these influences. Children who are brought up in the same home are usually different in personality and interests. Even though a child is influenced by his home life, he also has his own set of ambitions and goals in life, which he wants to fulfill. The way he fulfills his interests and desires may be outside a realm of which his parents approve.

We could list many other influences on the life of your child in addition to what has been mentioned already, but the point has been made sufficiently that your child needs more than a decent home life to live happily ever after. There is a constant battle raging for his mental, moral, and spiritual life.

Children will fulfill their parents' expectations if the parents are exceptionally strict with their children.

A third prevailing myth focuses on the strictness with which you rear your child. Many parents swing on pendulums. They look at other parents who have been ultrapermissive, and determine that permissiveness is not an acceptable child-rearing approach. So they hop the pendulum and swing to the other side of ultrastrictness. Some of these parents look to the Scriptures to back up their convictions, such as, "Train up a child in the way he should go, even when he is old he will not depart from it" (Prov. 22:6).

They believe that the only way to carry out this directive is to strangle their children with rules and regulations. They reason that by constant harping, preaching, and nagging at their children, they will reap positive responses from them. When the children do not behave properly, the parents inflict severe punishment.

Sadly, to the dismay of their parents, their children grow up with a bitter spirit and a rebellious life style, rather than a sweet spirit and a proper life style.

It is true that discipline is essential to rear a child with a healthy self-image and a loving spirit, but excessive punishment and unreasonable rules do not produce a spiritually mature individual. A fourth myth which parents should avoid as they rear their children concerns parental love.

Children understand parental love best through material gifts.

Many parents would deny that they are building upon such a philosophy, but their practice exposes their beliefs. Many parents find it easier to give their children things rather than to give them time. Some wives justify working "so that I can supplement my husband's income and provide nicer things for our children." It's not that children dislike the added material blessings. It's just that they don't accept material things as a demonstration of love. In fact, some children feel that they are being bought off with things.

How do children understand love? Love can be demonstrated in many ways, but here are three common ways to show love.

Show love through physical affection. The apostle Paul wrote
to the Thessalonian believers about his own affection for them.
In doing so, he used the affection of a mother for her child
as an object lesson of his love for the Thessalonian Christians.
He writes:

> But we proved to be gentle among you, as a nursing mother ten-
> derly cares for her own children. Having thus a fond affection
> for you, we were well pleased to impart to you not only the gospel,
> but also our own lives, because you had become very dear to us.
> For you recall, brethren, our labor and hardship, how working
> night and day so as not to be a burden to any of you, we proclaimed
> to you the gospel of God.
>
> 1 Thessalonians 2:7–9

Paul referred to a nursing mother tenderly caring for her
children. He talked about the mother giving her body to her
child, so that the child would be able to receive nourishment
and tender strokes. The child feels the warmth of the mother's
body, and the warm caress of her loving arms. The child knows
that he is loved when the mother touches, hugs, kisses, or
strokes him.

Show love through verbal affirmation. Too many children today grow up never hearing their mother or father say, "I love
you." Some parents may feel that it would seem silly. They
may be embarrassed to verbalize their love for their children,
but children, just like adults, need to hear verbal affirmation
of love.

Think of how many times God tells us, "I love you." We
not only need to hear these words from God when we've been
good, but especially when we know that we have disgraced
Him by taking matters into our own hands. When we feel
rejected and unloved, we need to hear what Paul wrote to
the Roman church:

> Who shall separate us from the love of Christ? Shall tribulation,
> or distress, or persecution, or famine, or nakedness, or peril, or
> sword? . . . For I am convinced that neither death, nor life, nor
> angels, nor principalities, nor things present, nor things to come,

nor powers, nor height, nor depth, nor any other created thing, shall be able to separate us from the love of God, which is in Christ Jesus our Lord.

Romans 8:35, 38–39

In addition to physical affection and verbal affirmation, there is a third way to demonstrate love.

Show love through time investment. One of the observations I have made as a parent of two teenage sons is that when your children begin to develop an affection for someone of the opposite sex, you don't have to teach them or plead with them to spend time with their boyfriend or girlfriend. In fact, I've come up with a new time principle. Through my observation I've concluded that "Time expands to fill the affection available." Growing love will always manifest itself in the willingness to spend time with the one you love.

God Himself has an unending love for you. That's why He promises you, "Let your way of life be free from the love of money, being content with what you have; for He Himself has said, 'I will never desert you, nor will I ever forsake you,' so that we confidently say, 'The Lord is my helper, I will not be afraid. What shall man do to me?'" (Heb. 13:5–6). Because of God's great love for you, He wants to spend time with you, and He wants you to spend time with Him.

Your child will know your love through physical affection, verbal affirmation, and the time you are willing to invest with him. Consider now another prevailing child-rearing myth.

Children by nature are interested in doing what is right.

There are those individuals who write books about allowing your child to grow up and experiment with life with little or no restrictions. Their basic thesis is that the child is inherently good; therefore, he will have a tendency to choose things that are good for him, as long as he is not restricted by having the parents' beliefs, values, and traditions placed upon him.

Again, both Scripture and experience prove the fallacy of this principle.

Biblical evidence is against this principle. Is the child born inherently good? Listen to the writer of Proverbs. "The rod and reproof give wisdom, but a child who gets his own way brings shame to his mother" (29:15). "Correct your son, and he will give you comfort; he will also delight your soul" (29:17). "Foolishness is bound up in the heart of a child; the rod of discipline will remove it far from him" (22:15). "He who spares his rod hates his son, but he who loves him disciplines him diligently" (13:24). Does this sound like inherent goodness? Certainly not!

Evaluate personal experience against this principle. Experience aptly demonstrates that children by nature are interested in doing what they want to do. Therefore, parents need to spend time helping them do what they should do.

Think of your own children. How often have you had to say, "No! Don't do that!"? Children are like curious, little puppies who put their noses to the ground and begin to track a scent. Unless they are stopped, they will eventually stray far away from where they should be.

I've never had to teach my children to dislike anyone. I've never had to teach my children to argue, or to become angry. All of that comes with the package of birth.

One further myth which I want to point out concerns the child's need for mother.

Children don't really need their mothers during early childhood, because child-care centers offer a convenient substitute.

As you see the tremendous increase in child-care centers around the country, it is obvious that many mothers are under the impression that such centers are good mother substitutes. I recognize that many mothers take their children to such places out of necessity, especially single parents. I'm also aware that such centers would provide a tremendous opportunity for churches to reach out to mothers who have to work. However, it is also important to recognize that child-care centers, whether in a church or totally secular, should never be seen as substitutes for the love and affection that a mother can give to her child. Jean Piaget, Co-Director of the Institute of Educational Science in Geneva, Switzerland, and Professor of Experimental Psychology at the University of Geneva, has conducted research for more than forty years into the origin and development of cognitive structures and moral judgment in the early years of life. His studies on the moral judgment of the child were first published in 1932. Some of Piaget's studies indicate that adequate mother substitutes are all right for the first six months or so of life, but that on the social level, the mother is very specifically needed by about seven months of age. In other words, before the child is seven or eight months of age, another competent person can be substituted for the mother without any serious consequences, but not very readily after that age (*Christian Child Rearing and Personality Development,* Dr. Paul D. Meier, p. 117).

Likewise, Dr. James Dobson emphasizes the fact that the mother-child relationship is absolutely vital to healthy development of children. He says, "Children cannot raise themselves properly. This fact was illustrated again in a recent conversation with a research psychologist who visited my office. He had been studying the early childhoods of inmates at a state prison in Arizona. He and his associates were seeking to discover the common characteristics which the prisoners shared, hoping to unlock the causes for their antisocial behavior. It was initially assumed that poverty would be the common thread, but their findings contradicted these expectations. The inmates came from all socio-economic levels of society, though most of them attempted to excuse their crimes by professing to have been poor. Instead, researchers discovered one fundamental characteristic shared by the men: an absence of adult contact in their early home lives. As children, they spent most of their time in the company of their peers—or altogether alone. Such was the childhood of Lee Harvey Oswald, Charles Manson, and many other perpetrators of violent crimes later in life. The conclusion is inescapable: there is no substitute for loving parental leadership in the early development of children" (*Dr. Dobson Answers Your Questions,* pp. 358–359).

Mother, as you commit yourself to rearing your children effectively, don't buy into these prevailing child-rearing myths. They'll create only greater problems. Let's go a step further. Since we're talking about rearing children by using your time wisely, consider further some practical time-management principles as you rear your children.

Adopt Practical Time-Management Principles in Your Child Rearing

I've selected the following time-management principles for your study and adoption.

Observe your children's uniqueness.

Have you taken the time to observe carefully each of your children's unique qualities? No two children are alike. I don't believe anyone who does not know our family would conclude that our two sons are brothers. They do not look alike, their personalities are not the same, and many of their interests are different. Therefore, it would have been foolish for my wife and I to have tried to conform the one to the image of the other. Likewise, your children differ in personality, ability, and interest. It's going to take time to carefully observe those differences, so that when you set specific goals for each child, those goals will match his uniqueness. And that's the next step.

Set some basic child-rearing goals for each child.

Building a child is something like building a house. You decide what you want, draw up the plans, gather the resources, and make adjustments as the house is being built. Likewise, before you can build your child's life, you have to decide what you want.

One of the women in our church, Carol Rischer, has established a plan of action for each one of her children. She explained the plan of action to me in the following manner: Carol keeps a journal on her family, devoting one chapter to each child. The chapters include specific goals for each child in a variety of areas. For example, she has established spiritual goals, such as reading Scripture, praying every day, and attending family devotions every morning; physical goals—taking swimming lessons for two weeks every summer; musical goals—practicing the piano and the violin every day for a specified length of time; educational goals—preparing the child for college and discussing it with her, even while she is young; social goals—planning family activities and interacting with others. Carol reviews these goals weekly and prepares a schedule according to determined priorities.

What do you want your children to become? Well, consider the following possible goals.

Develop character goals. Many parents are concerned about their children's reputation, but they should be even more concerned about their children's character. Reputation is what people *think* you are, while character is what you really are.

A child needs to be taught how to give to others. By nature, man is basically selfish and desires to take and receive. That's why the apostle Paul's philosophy "It is more blessed to give than to receive" makes very little sense to most people. Most individuals are taught by instruction or observation that it is more blessed to receive than to give!

Parents also need to teach their children to be loving toward others. Because self-esteem is very fragile, and can often be crushed during the early childhood years through sibling rivalry and ridicule, it is imperative that parents teach their children to love one another. Dobson says, "Adults who take the time to cultivate that sensitivity can create a genuine empathy for the handicapped child, the overweight child, the unattractive child, the retarded child, or the younger child" (*Dr. Dobson Answers Your Questions,* p. 500).

Character development is essential for a healthy adult life. Dr. Paul Meier emphasizes this need by writing in *Christian Child Rearing and Personality Development:* "What a difference it would make if parents would primarily praise their child's good character and behavior! Character and behavior defects are correctable! Physical defects usually are not. A child whose parents value and praise good character and behavior will strive to improve his or her character and behavioral weaknesses in order to gain both parental approval and feelings of self-worth, which are vital to good mental health" (p. 10).

Develop skill goals. Many children have hidden musical, athletic, or mechanical talents. It is imperative that mothers observe the surfacing of these skills, and provide opportunities for their children to develop such skills. Since our own family enjoyed music, and my mother was a soloist in our church, it was natural for her to seek the same skills in my own life. Therefore, when I was in fourth grade, I began to take clarinet lessons. From that point I learned to play other instruments, and also took vocal lessons. Though I never excelled musically, I have come to appreciate music greatly.

Likewise, my athletic aptitudes were developed during my childhood years at the YMCA. Both my parents encouraged me to join the Y, where I spent many evenings and Saturday mornings developing my interests and skills in athletics.

Mother, is your child naturally attracted to athletics, music, or building things with his hands? If so, spend time with him and encourage him to develop in those areas of his life. This may include endless hours of taxi-ing your children to soccer games, school plays, piano recitals, and so forth, but the dividends will pay handsomely in the end. Along with character and skill goals, it's important to include the next objective.

Develop attitude goals. Your children will develop various attitudes toward people and things. And mother, you have a tremendous privilege and responsibility to shape your child's attitude. What kind of attitude do you want your child to have toward authority? Toward siblings? Toward God? Toward others? Toward himself? Most attitudes are caught, rather than taught. Their attitudes are often reflective of what they see around them. The attitudes you model will be attitudes which your children may assimilate. Next, let's discuss the establishment of important social objectives.

Develop social goals. Do you have any social goals for your child? Do you want him to get along with people? Then you need to take time to help your child enjoy the presence of other people. If your child is socially shy, you have the opportunity to help him grow out of that shyness.

One of the mistakes I've seen mothers make is to always talk for their children in social settings. For instance, a mother and child walk into a room. Someone looks down at the child and says, "Hi, Johnny! What are you doing here today?" As Johnny looks up at the stranger and opens his mouth to speak, his mother immediately steps in and answers the question.

Another mistake I see made, happens when several women get together in a home for a social gathering. As they are talking, little Johnny comes running into the room to share some new discovery with his mother. As Johnny interrupts the conversation and shows his mother what he has just found outside in the backyard, mother immediately responds with, "Johnny, go outside and play. Can't you see I'm busy? You know that it's impolite to interrupt people!" As this scene is reinforced over the years, Johnny learns that social gatherings are not for him, so he finds solace just being by himself.

Other goals could be added to the list, such as *career goals, value goals,* and *spiritual goals,* but what is important is that you have some goals toward which you are working, because they help keep you on track, and facilitate your decisions concerning the best area in which to invest time with your children.

Now as you observe your children's uniqueness and begin setting some child-rearing goals for each child, you need to also organize yourself to reach those goals.

Get yourself organized in order to reach those goals.

Many people have goals in their minds, but the goals become nothing but empty dreams. Why? Because these people never get themselves organized. By organizing, I mean first to set priorities for those goals, and then set a schedule as to when you expect to reach those goals.

Set your goal priorities. It's obvious that you cannot accomplish everything you want to do in a short period of time. Some of your goals must be long-range, while others will be short-range. You will be able to accomplish some goals in a few weeks, while others will take months and even years to complete. Therefore, you must decide which goals are important at the various stages of your child's life.

I know parents who observed natural athletic ability in their child at an early age. They also recognized that by the time that child was college age, the expense of his education would be almost prohibitive. Therefore, they've invested a lot of time and money to help that child develop his athletic abilities. And when he became of college age, he received several scholarships to play for the college team. Other parents have done the same thing in the areas of musical and academic abilities, but priorities without a schedule are useless.

Schedule your goals by organizing yourself. Let's say that as a Christian, your primary goal is your child's spiritual development. You want your child to know Jesus Christ as personal Savior early in life. You also desire that your child grows in knowledge of the Scriptures. Therefore, you will spend time scheduling your week so that your child will have an opportunity to attend Sunday school and church, as well as weekday activities at church. You will spend time helping him memorize Bible verses. You will invest time praying for your child, and consistently model a Christian life style for him. Spiritual development is a high priority for your child, and so you schedule yourself accordingly.

You may also see music as a high priority for your child's development. Therefore, you will schedule your week, so that your child can take lessons. You will also schedule time to attend recitals, concerts, and other musical activities in which your child will be involved.

So as you begin to manage your time properly, you will observe your child's uniqueness, set child-rearing goals, and organize yourself so that you can reach those goals. Along with these principles, there is one further step.

Discipline yourself to achieve those goals.

Discipline is merely saying *yes* to one option, and *no* to another. This may mean that you choose not to work outside the home while your children are young. It may include resisting the temptation of getting too overly involved in volunteer work while your children are still young. It may also mean turning down various opportunities, which you would like to accept for your own personal growth, until the children are older.

Just as the athlete needs to discipline himself in order to become a better athlete, and the musician needs to discipline himself to become a more proficient musician, so does the mother need to discipline herself to become a more effective mother. Self-discipline is not easy because we all have desires that crave satisfaction. However, as we look at the long-range goal of developing a mature child, the small sacrifices which we must make along the way will seem insignificant.

Up to this point, I've said that there are three principles which can help you become a more effective mother. *The first one was not buying into the prevailing child-rearing myths. The second focused on adopting practical time-management principles for child rearing.* Consider now the third principle.

Commit Yourself to Whatever Time It Takes to Be an Effective Mother

I want to suggest these specific areas for which you need to carve time.

Take time to pray for your children.

Prayer can be an extremely effective tool to accomplish some of those goals for your child. I remember reading *The Confessions of Saint Augustine* many years ago. In this book, he praised his mother, Monica, who prayed daily that God would touch her son's heart and turn him to the living Christ. Augustine himself had very little interest in Christianity. He was controlled by fleshly desires. Although suffering from moral guilt, he still saw no value in turning to Christianity. But his mother continued to pray. One day Augustine read these words from the Book of Romans, "Let us behave properly as in the day, not in carousing and drunkenness, not in sexual promiscuity and sensuality, not in strife and jealousy. But put on the Lord Jesus Christ, and make no provision for the flesh in regard to its lusts" (Rom. 13:13–14). At that point, Augustine turned his heart over to Jesus Christ, eventually becoming a great teacher and theologian in the church. But prayer alone does not develop great relationships between parent and child. Recreation is also important.

Take time to play with your children.

Children who are brought up in homes where there is a strong emphasis on Bible reading, prayer, and church attendance, but little or no emphasis on playing and laughing together, do not grow up enjoying the things of God.

A family should be fun. Children should know that Mom and Dad enjoy playing with them. My wife and I decided to divide up the types of games we would play with our children, because of our own personal interests. Therefore, I would take the boys outside to play football, soccer, or to wrestle with them on the floor. My wife, however, enjoyed puzzles and table games. The boys were not concerned about who played what. They appreciated the fact that both mom and dad played with them. Then add teaching to your praying and playing.

Take time to instruct your children.

Children learn best when they hear, see, and do. Children love it when their parents tell them stories at bedtime. They also love to act out the stories and to look at the big pictures time and again.

Mothers will find many teachable moments during the day, especially when children ask them questions. Those special times are excellent teachable moments, and a mother needs to be conscious of such opportunities. Still another time investment is to pay attention to what is said.

Take time to listen to your children.

Mothers have a tendency to tell their children what to do and what not to do. This is important, but it's equally important to listen to what the children are saying to you. You must listen to what they do not say, as well as what they do tell you. At times you'll have to question your children for more information. It's important that your children know that they can always come to you and express what's on their hearts, without fearing reprimands or put-downs.

I've always appreciated my wife's inquisitive spirit. Over the years as our children came in the house, she would inquire, "Tell me what your day was like." Or, "What did you do at school today?" Be a good listener. Your children have a lot to share. One more time investment concerns your own further education in child rearing.

Take time to learn more about child rearing.

Effective child rearing does not come automatically. There is so much to know about how children learn; what makes one child different from another; why children do the things they do, and so on. Child rearing is a full-time responsibility, and cannot be learned in a short time span.

There are many good books and cassette tapes which are available on the subject of child rearing. I strongly encourage you to take advantage of those materials, so that you can learn how to become a more effective mother. I've listed a number of books at the end of this book.

Conclusion

In conclusion, consider three specific questions and project your mind and your family's future.

1. What kind of relationship do you want to have with your child when he or she is a teenager? List several characteristics which you envision.

2. What basic information do you believe you should impart to your child? (Include spiritual, social, financial, world view and other facts.)

3. What type of family life do you want your child to have when he or she is married? (Consider helping your children

think through what they want in a mate: character, occupation, spiritual development, personality.)

Whatever answers you come up with, I guarantee that those results will not be accomplished by chance or by osmosis. They need to be established as *goals.* They are going to take time. And if you are willing to invest the time, I know that God is willing to pay great dividends on your investment.

Effective mothering does not just happen, it takes time. Let's close this chapter with the encouraging words of the apostle Paul who wrote: "And let us not lose heart in doing good, for in due time we shall reap if we do not grow weary" (Gal. 6:9).

8

Why You Must Spend Time with Your Spouse

Introduction

The law of Moses contained many laws other than the Ten Commandments. And one such law tucked away in the Book of Deuteronomy deals with the issue of military exemption. The first two individuals who are exempt temporarily from military duty include the man who has built a new house, but has not yet dedicated it, and the man who has planted a vineyard, but has not been able to eat of its fruit. Then note two other individuals who are temporarily exempt from military duty: "And who is the man that is engaged to a woman and has not married her? Let him depart and return to his house, lest he die in the battle and another man marry her. . . . When a man takes a new wife, he shall not go out with the army, nor be charged with any duty; he shall be free at home one year and shall give happiness to his wife whom he has taken" (Deut. 20:7; 24:5).

Why such an exemption? Because building a relationship takes time. A marriage may be consummated on the first night, but a successful marriage needs time for each partner to know one another—time to adjust—time to give and receive love—time to work out those little incompatibilities. Read on and discover in more detail why time together is essential for the health of a marital relationship.

Too Many Marriage Relationships Are Unfruitful

In the Gospel of Luke, Jesus tells a parable about four types of soil (heart condition) upon which the seed (the Scriptures) falls: a hardened soil, a rocky soil, a thorny soil, and a fertile soil. These same four characteristics can also depict the various relationships of marriage.

Some marital relationships are hardened.

Jesus says, "The sower went out to sow his seed; and as he sowed, some fell beside the road; and it was trampled under foot, and the birds of the air devoured it" (Luke 8:5).

This could represent those marriages in which one or both mates feel as if they are constantly being trampled upon. It might be a husband who can never do enough to please his wife. She puts him down for everything, and whenever he does succeed in something, she reminds him of his past failures or former poor decisions. He becomes embittered and angry. He erects a protective shell around himself as a defense against her put-downs. This marriage unfortunately illustrates the Proverb, "A constant dripping on a day of steady rain and a contentious woman are alike" (27:15).

Perhaps the spouse feeling trampled upon is the wife whose husband acts like a tyrant. He constantly cracks jokes about her, emphasizing her inabilities and physical defects. He enjoys controlling her and using her for his sexual pleasure. This husband totally disregards the biblical injunction that states, "You husbands likewise, live with your wives in an understanding way, as with a weaker vessel, since she is a woman; and grant her honor as a fellow-heir of the grace of life, so that your prayers may not be hindered" (1 Peter 3:7).

She, in turn, reacts to his abuses by harboring feelings of

hate, anger, or resentment. She channels her energy away from trying to improve their strained relationship, and directs that energy towards either defensive or offensive purposes. The relationship soon deteriorates into a hardness of heart.

Some marital relationships are rocky.

"And other seed fell on rocky soil, and as soon as it grew up, it withered away, because it had no moisture. . . . And those in the rocky soil are those who, when they hear, receive the word with joy; and then have no firm root; they believe for a while, and in time of temptation fall away" (Luke 8:6, 13).

A "rocky marriage" refers to a relationship full of problems with a questionable outcome. The underlying problem is the shallowness of the relationship. There is so little to hold the marriage together, that these couples usually terminate the marriage in a divorce court.

Some of these relationships get started with the wrong motive or under very poor circumstances. They may begin with an overphysical attraction; or sometimes these marriages are forced due to an unexpected pregnancy. Others result from wanting to get out from under parental authority. Another type of rocky marriage is the second marriage, wherein a spouse has been hurt through a divorce and is seeking security and companionship in the new mate. Or perhaps the individual uses the new marriage as a weapon to get even with the former spouse.

Whatever the cause, this marital relationship has no depth. Therefore, when too many pressures, exorbitant amounts of stress or some catastrophic event occurs in that home, there is not enough substance to keep the marriage together.

Some marital relationships are thorny.

These relationships are described in the following statement: "And other seed fell among the thorns; and the thorns grew up with it, and choked it out . . . . And the seed which fell among the thorns, these are the ones who have heard, and as they go on their way, they are choked with worries and riches and pleasures of this life, and bring no fruit to maturity" (Luke 8:7, 14).

Such marriages are plagued with three major problems: worries, riches, and pleasures. The mates worry about not having enough money, or they fight over how the money is being spent. Some husbands get so wrapped up in their personal pursuits of pleasure, that they neglect their wives and children. And in our sex-crazed society, infidelity is almost commonplace.

Some marital relationships are fruitful.

"And other seed fell into the good ground, and grew up, and produced a crop a hundred times as great . . . . And the seed in the good ground, these are the ones who have heard the word in an honest and good heart, and hold it fast, and bear fruit with perseverance" (Luke 8:8, 15).

This marriage bears four distinctive characteristics: *honesty, goodness, commitment,* and *perseverance.*

The relationship is honest and open.   So many relationships are filled with conniving, hidden agendas, and manipulative tactics in order to get one's own way. Isaac and Rebekah did not have an honest relationship. When Isaac was old and could barely see, Rebekah took advantage of his problem and manipulated events, so that Isaac would give his patriarchal blessing to Jacob, rather than to Esau, his firstborn. Her plan included dressing Jacob in Esau's clothes, so that old Isaac would think he was blessing Esau. With Rebekah's conniving and Jacob's lying to his father, the blessing was given to him rather than to Esau.

Today many husbands and wives attempt to deceive one another in order to get what they want. Such a relationship will never become fruitful. Fruitfulness is the result of being willing to open up to one another, to share your innermost thoughts and feelings with your spouse.

The relationship builds upon goodness of heart. How would a good-hearted husband relate to his wife? He would be willing to forgive; have an interest in her needs and desires; and be willing to put up with her idiosyncracies. He also would be open to change those areas of his life which conflicted with what was best for the marriage. He would be faithful in his responsibilities. His wife would not have to worry about his moral character.

The relationship includes a commitment for life. The marriage that bears fruit is one which removes the option of divorce. The individuals take their vows seriously, when they take each other for better or for worse. They don't demand that the other person does all the changing. They don't demand perfection from their mate. Despite the problems, the hurts, the tears, and tensions, they remain committed to one another.

The relationship includes perseverance. Perseverance is that ability to stick to a course of action, no matter what problems you encounter. Whereas commitment says, "I will," perseverance is able to say, "I'm still committed."

According to the Bible, perseverance is the vital link between problems and mature character. Everyone has problems, but everyone is not mature in his character or attitudes. But perseverance bridges the gap between the two. Paul writes, ". . . tribulation brings about perseverance; and perseverance, proven character . . ." (Rom. 5:3–4).

Where there have been strong arguments, abuse, perhaps even infidelity, divorce is often around the corner; but perseverance seeks a solution and refuses to give up, resulting in a marriage which bears much fruit.

However, the faithful marriage has become the exception, rather than the rule, because you must want to take the time and pay the price to build such a solid and growing relationship.

There is a major increase in the divorce rate.

Another reason why it is essential to spend time with your spouse is not only because the majority of marriages are not fruitful relationships, but also because of the major increase in the divorce rate. Consider these staggering facts about the increase of divorce in the USA. In 1960, there were 25 divorces for every 100 marriages in America. In 1975, the rate jumped to 48 divorces per 100 marriages. And at the present rate of increase, there will be 63 divorces for every 100 marriages by 1990 (*Strike the Original Match,* Charles Swindoll, pp. 39–40).

When you look at these figures from the perspective of the innocent children who have to bear the emotional scars and consequences of divorce, the picture is bleak. ". . . Between 1970 and 1981, the proportion of children living with only one parent jumped from 11 to 19 percent, and the number of one parent families soared from 3.3 million to 6.6 million. More than one million youngsters a year live through the shocks of a marital breakup. 'Today's children are the first generation in the country's history who think divorce and separation are a normal part of family life,' says sociologist Andrew Cherlin of Johns Hopkins University" (*U.S. News & World Report,* Aug. 9, 1982).

Why is there such a high divorce rate, especially among Christians? In his book *Strike the Original Match,* Chuck Swindoll has boiled it down to four reasons:

1. *Public Opinion*—"Everybody does it."

2. *Accommodating Theology*—fitting the Bible into our own life style. Instead of placing ourselves under its authority and doing what it says, we justify our actions and then look for loopholes in Scripture to back up our life style.

Interestingly enough, the devil is a master of using biblical texts for his own purposes. When tempting Jesus, Satan quoted Scripture to the Lord, implying that He would not have to worry about suffering any consequences for disobedience to God.

Then the devil took Him into the holy city, and he stood Him on the pinnacle of the temple, and said to Him, "If you are the Son of God, throw Yourself down; for it is written, 'He will give His angels charge concerning you; and on their hands they will bear you up, lest you strike your foot against a stone.' Jesus said to him, "On the other hand, it is written, 'You shall not tempt the Lord your God.' "

Matthew 4:5–7

So today a husband or wife may rationalize, "God wants me to be happy. And as long as I'm married to that person, I'll never be happy. Therefore, I'll get a divorce and marry a beautiful Christian woman [or a handsome Christian man]. Then I'll be happy and at the same time please God."

In *Strike the Original Match* Swindoll relates his own frustration as he attempted in vain over a three-year period to persuade ten Christian couples to remain together. He writes:

In each case one of the mates in each marriage has willfully (and skillfully) accommodated his or her theology, so that the Scriptures actually "approved" their plan to walk out. There were no ugly fights or bold public announcements like, "I am denying the faith!" No need for that. Calmly and with reserved respectability, they simply left. That's it. Against my counsel and strong efforts to stop them. Against scriptural injunctions. Against their mates' desires. In spite of the certain danger to their children, and regardless of the shame it brought against the name of God and the church of Jesus Christ.

Hang on—not one seems to be wrestling with much guilt or personal shame. In fact, several say they have never been happier. A few openly insist they are closer to the Lord than ever before in their lives. Some are still engaged in public ministries (p. 156).

3. *Delayed Consequences* is the third reason for the rise in divorce. In other words, because God doesn't zap them immediately, they think they've gotten away with something. They conclude: *That wasn't so bad after all. I thought that God would be angry with me and make me feel miserable. But actually, I feel pretty good.*

Solomon wrote, "Because the sentence against an evil deed is not executed quickly, therefore the hearts of the sons of men among them are given fully to do evil" (Eccl. 8:11). On the other hand, the Bible unequivocally states, "Do not be deceived, God is not mocked; for whatever a man sows, that he will also reap" (Gal. 6:7). There is always a time interval between reaping and sowing, but I guarantee, there will not be a crop failure. You will reap what you've sown, even if the interval may take several years.

4. *Christian Approval.* This is the final reason for an upward trend in the divorce rate. At one time the church took a strong stand on the divorce issue, but since the problem has crept into the pews of the sanctuary, it has been met with a barrage of silence. Therefore, many Christians conclude, "Because the church hasn't taken a stand on divorce, I'll get a divorce until they do." Or, "I guess divorce is okay after all, because I never hear anything said against it from the pulpit."

Well, God has never changed His mind on the issue. If you think for one moment that God has gotten soft on the problem, listen to His scathing rebuke of the nation Israel through the prophet Malachi:

> "And this is another thing you do: you cover the altar of the Lord with tears, with weeping and with groaning, because He no longer regards the offering or accepts it with favor for your hand. Yet you say, 'For what reason?' Because the Lord has been a witness between you and the wife of your youth, against whom you have dealt treacherously, though she is your companion and your wife by covenant. . . . 'For I hate divorce,' says the Lord God of Israel . . . So take heed to your spirit, that you do not deal treacherously. You have wearied the Lord with your words. Yet you say, 'How have we wearied Him?' In that you say, "Everyone who does evil is good in the sight of the Lord, and He delights in them," or "Where is the God of justice?"
>
> Malachi 2:13–14, 16–17

Because of this terrible rise in divorce, and because many marriage relationships are not fruitful relationships, it is essential to spend the necessary time together and make your marriage work. Now consider a third reason why time with your spouse is important.

The Expectations of Young Couples

One of the questions normally asked in premarital counseling is, "What do you expect out of this marriage?" The responses are usually somewhat humorous and border more on fiction than reality. Four common expectations include: eternal romance, immediate financial security, an unending open communication, and the certainty of changing the other person into conforming to one's image of the perfect husband or wife.

Some young couples expect eternal romance.

Most young couples would not come right out and say that their marriage will be problem-free. *Intellectually* they expect disagreements, arguments, and misunderstandings. *Emotionally,* however, they feel that they might be able to beat the odds because they are so much in love. Marriage from an emotional standpoint is often perceived as one long date, culminating nightly in a blissful sexual union. That bubble often pops on the wedding night, and the fairy-tale marriage begins its journey into the world of reality.

I am not implying that romantic love has to cease as the marital relationship matures. To the contrary, romantic love is essential for a healthy marriage, but the difference between this love at the courtship level and ten years later is that during the courtship period, romance is almost automatic. Everything is still new and fresh. Just a glance across the classroom at an attractive girl can turn a guy on. Holding hands with a cute guy sends chills through a girl's emotional system.

I never did very well in chemistry during my high-school days, because while I was supposed to be working on an experiment, I'd find myself looking out the window watching the girls' gym class play field hockey. There was this one special girl whom I had met a few months earlier. Just running up and down the field with a hockey stick in her hand, she was able to do something to my own chemistry. For some strange reason, chemistry class just couldn't compete with the attraction out the window. Though I barely passed my chemistry class, I got an *A+* on my other pursuit, because I ended up marrying that pleasant diversion.

Romantic love. Easy and natural in the beginning of a relationship. However, when the responsibilities and realities of life confront you day after day, it takes time and effort to keep the romantic flame burning.

Some young couples expect financial security early in their marriage.

I do not want to imply that young couples expect that attaining a certain standard of living will be easy. It's just that they see little reason why they can't live on the same economic level as their parents at a very early period of life. They fail to consider that their parents spent twenty or thirty years to reach their economic standard of living.

Many young couples immediately want to own a home as large, if not larger, than their parents. They want to drive a new car, eat out at the fine restaurants, and travel wherever they so desire. So when they awaken to the reality of a huge debt which restricts their freedom to eat out, travel, and buy whatever they wish, the myth of financial security turns back into a pumpkin. Each begins to feel that his spouse needs to cut back in the spending and make sacrifices. And this works, until one of the partners thinks that his privileges or rights are being violated. Then the fireworks begin.

Managing money wisely takes time. It demands a willingness to compromise; a concern for each other's needs; and great wisdom in setting financial goals which are mutually satisfactory. This leads to a third expectation of young couples—which does not materialize without the necessary time to make it happen—open communication.

Some young couples expect automatic open communication.

During the courtship years, a young couple does a lot of talking. They learn of each other's interests, family history, likes, and dislikes. They enjoy staying out to the wee hours of the morning, talking until they can barely keep their eyes open. And so it is natural to expect that marriage will be an extended conversation.

However, after the early months of marriage, communication often shows some signs of lessening. Busyness engulfs the couple to the point that when they are together, one or both may be too tired to carry on an intelligent conversation. In fact, the lack of communication is one of the greatest problems in contemporary marriages.

"In a four-year study, hundreds of marriage counselors were asked to list the main causes of marriage troubles among couples in counseling. 35% of the difficulties were over children, sex, money, leisure, relatives, and infidelity. But 86% complained, 'We can't talk to each other' " (*Dad's Only*, September 1981).

Usually, it's the wife who desperately craves conversation with her husband, because she has been at home with the children all day. However, he has been dealing with people all day and wants to come home and escape the conversation. His great desire is to be left alone—at least for a period of time—so that he can wind down from the rat race. So he may hide behind the newspaper, grunting periodically in response to his wife's lively monologue. In most marriages, communication needs resuscitation desperately, and this can be achieved only by spending time with one another.

Some young couples expect to change their spouse after marriage.

A fourth common expectation of young couples is the assumption that any present idiosyncracy or weakness of a spouse can easily be changed after the "I dos." I've counseled too many starry-eyed young Christians who were about to enter a marital relationship with an unbeliever on the assumption that, "Oh, I know he'll trust Christ after we get married. He already promised me that he would start coming to church after our honeymoon." Others have related, "I know she's really a messy housekeeper, but since I'm a perfectionist I'll make sure she keeps the house in perfect shape."

The only person you can change is yourself. Your partner may also change over the years, but not by coercing or threatening. The apostle Peter counseled wives who had become Christians before their husbands that the way to win him to the Lord is to replace preaching at him with modeling a godly life style before him:

> In the same way, you wives, be submissive to your own husbands, so that even if any of them are disobedient to the word, they may be won without a word by the behavior of their wives, as they observe your chaste and respectful behavior. And let not your adornment be external only—braiding the hair, and wearing gold jewelry, and putting on dresses; but let it be the hidden person of the heart, with the imperishable quality of a gentle and quiet spirit, which is precious in the sight of God.
>
> 1 Peter 3:1–4

The imperfections which are evident before marriage will become much more noticeable after marriage. However, when each partner is willing to take the time to talk through and work through those imperfections in character, beliefs, and attitudes, change is possible.

Many Time Demands Hinder a Fruitful Relationship

A fourth reason why spending time with each other is essential emerges from the many time demands, which hinder a growing and fruitful relationship.

Work demands one's time.

After those blissful first few months of marriage, the husband begins to spend more time on his job. He realizes that he is low man on the totem pole. He knows that if he is going to advance, he'll need to prove himself—and that demands time. He may decide to work a few more hours than the others. Or he might decide to attend some seminars on his own time, in order to gain a better understanding about his specific job.

Work is the extension of the man. Not only does it provide the base for financial security, but it also is his means to measure self-worth. The husband will often determine his self-worth by what he has been able to achieve in his work. Some men also measure their personal value by how much money they can earn, or by their position and title in the company. Others measure self-worth by the number of promotions gained, by what others think of his job, or by how creative he is on the job.

On the other hand, the home is usually the extension of the woman. Women often feel that their house is a reflection of themselves. That is why many housewives climb the walls when they watch their husbands kick off their shoes and leave them lying in the living room, or let dirty underwear and socks lie in the middle of the bedroom. A messy house makes many women feel messy.

However, with the tremendous increase of women in the work force, the picture is beginning to change. For some women, their job has become the extension of themselves. And many women are starting to measure their self-worth by the way they are able to compete with the men in the work force. And when both husband and wife are competing in the work force, time together becomes even more scarce.

In a recent *U.S. News & World Report* article, the writer states, "For many two-career households, which are expected to grow in the 1980s, the scarcest commodity is not money, but time . . ." (9 August 1982, p. 28).

Children demand one's time.

But if work occupies most of the husband's available time, and possibly that of the wife, the other time user is the child.

When the first child arrives on the scene, most mothers quit work for a period of time. Of course, the single parent seldom has that luxury. The more the wife concentrates large amounts of time on her children, her husband focuses his time on his job and hobbies.

This is when the drift begins to emerge. Neither partner plans to spend less time with one another. It just seems to work out that way.

If such neglect of one another continues over a period of years, common interests between husband and wife dwindle; communication evaporates into a faint echo; and without realizing it, the empty-nest years appear on the horizon with two strangers living under a common roof.

Conclusion

Spending time with your spouse can not be considered a luxury. Instead it must be perceived as the lifeblood of your marital relationship. And because few couples use their time to build that relationship, many of America's marriages are anemic. Some marriages are even in need of an emergency transfusion.

In the next chapter, I will discuss how to carve prime time out of your busy twenty-four-hour day—and invest it in getting to know one another.

Before you turn to the next chapter, answer the questions on the next page in light of your present marital relationship. How are your vital signs? Check them out yourself.

1. Rate your relationship with spouse.	1 2 3 Poor	4 5 Fair	6 7 8 Good	9 10 Excellent
2. Estimate the amount of time with spouse.	1 2 3 Very Little	4 5 Some	6 7 8 Adequate	9 10 A Lot
3. Evaluate the quality of time with spouse.	1 2 3 Boring	4 5 O.K.	6 7 8 Usually Enjoyable	9 10 Terrific
4. Determine the degree of commitment you have to work on your time problems with spouse.	1 2 3 Little to None	4 5 Might Try	6 7 8 Hope to Improve	9 10 Total Commit-ment

9

Making the Most of Your Time Together

Introduction

After the wedding, every newlywed wants to live happily ever after. For almost half of those couples, however, their dream is just that—a dream. They begin with saying, "I do," but eventually say, "I no longer do." There are many reasons why these marriages don't blossom into fruitful relationships, but the one hindrance we will focus on is the failure to spend time cultivating togetherness.

In the last chapter, you learned why couples need to invest time with one another. This chapter will help you gain insight into how you can make time for your spouse, and what you can do when you are together. Consider first how to carve out of a busy schedule the necessary time for growing a productive relationship.

How Can a Couple Make Time to Be Together?

Make time together a higher priority.

Parkinson's Law states that "work expands to fill the time available." If time together remains a mere option, rather than a necessity, many activities will divert you from spending time with your spouse. Often church activities become the greatest culprit. Husbands and wives may become engrossed in Bible studies, Sunday school, missionary endeavors, evangelistic out-reaches, and committee meetings. Some couples are willing to sacrifice their time together for the sake of serving God. The idea has some merit, but it can be taken to extremes. The devil has used this busyness many times, putting a wedge between a husband-wife relationship.

Consider for instance an attractive Christian woman in the church choir who becomes infatuated with the choir director. They begin to spend time together after the rehearsals "to talk about the music for next Sunday." And the more they are together, the deeper the infatuation, until they commit themselves to each other physically and emotionally and even-tually leave their mates, convincing themselves it must be of God.

James clearly states, "Let no one say when he is tempted, 'I am being tempted by God'; for God cannot be tempted by evil, and He Himself does not tempt any one" (James 1:13). James goes on to say that the temptation comes from our own lusts (v. 14). When we take time from our spouse to spend with someone of the opposite sex, even though we are involved in church activities, we may become the victims of our lust.

The apostle Peter encouraged wives to model spirituality before their husbands. That implies the need to take time with their husbands, so that they can see their changed lives . . . "they may be won without a word by the behavior of their wives, as they *observe* your chaste and respectful behavior" (1 Peter 3:1–2, *italics added*). Time together must take a higher priority in most homes.

Once time together becomes important enough to you, you'll find many ways to make it a reality, but placing togetherness higher on your priority list is merely a first step.

Set aside a specific time each week for togetherness.

When our family went on a three-week vacation several years ago, the lawn at our house was immaculate. The grass was well groomed, the weeds had been pulled, and the bushes trimmed. But when we returned, the lawn was full of crab grass. Weeds were growing in the flower beds. The bushes looked like huge "pac men" ready to consume the house. I was reminded of the Proverb about the sluggard: "I passed by the field of the sluggard, and by the vineyard of the man lacking sense; and behold, it was completely overgrown with thistles; its surface was covered with nettles, and its stone wall was broken down. When I saw, I reflected upon it; I looked and received instruction. 'A little sleep, a little slumber, a little folding of the hands to rest,' Then your poverty will come as a robber, and your want like an armed man" (Prov 24:30–34)

A sluggish marital relationship reflects the same image. The couple neglects to trim the excess problems in their relationship, or pull the weeds of discontent, bitterness, jealousy, misunderstanding, and resentment, resulting in an impoverished relationship. However, when a couple constantly makes time during the week for each other, the misunderstandings or hurt feelings can be brought out into the open and nipped in the bud, before they enlarge and choke the romance from the marriage. How can you get started? Begin with your calendar.

Use a calendar to mark off every Thursday night, Friday night, or Saturday night as "Spouse Night." Now that is different from Family Night when you include the children. This is a special time for you and your spouse. Then when somebody invites you to go out that night or to do some volunteer work, you can reply with honesty, "Sorry, I'll be busy Thursday evening. Perhaps some other time."

Now some Christians feel that this would be deceptive. In fact, they believe that time with one's spouse should always be sacrificed at the altar of church work or some other worthy endeavor.

I disagree. The Book of Ecclesiastes says that there is a time for everything. One of those activities is an opportunity to be with your spouse. And one of the best services you can render to another person is to model a loving marital relationship to an unloving and confused world. And that takes time.

Linda and I have chosen Saturdays as our "Spouse Day." We spend more hours together on Saturday than any other time during the week. Usually we go out for breakfast. Later we may shop, or take a drive in the country, or come back to the house and relax. But the day belongs to each other.

Include one another in your recreational activities.

Some couples get themselves entrapped in a hobby or activity which occupies so much time, they have little time remaining to be with their spouse. Dr. Howard Hendricks recalls how he used to enjoy playing golf several times a week. One day he awakened to the fact that he was taking too much time away from his family, so he put his clubs aside and invested the time with his family.

I am not implying that there is anything wrong with enjoying such activities with others, or even by yourself. Too often, however, the spouse is excluded from leisure activities. Here are some possibilities.

One couple enjoys camping together. Another plays various sports together, such as golf, racquetball, jogging, swimming, or walking. When Linda and I lived in Minneapolis, we often walked together, especially during the fall season. We'd walk through the woods along the Mississippi River, inhaling the fragrance carried by the cool breeze; crunching the colorful leaves beneath our feet. Another couple may enroll together in a night class at the university, while another one chooses to attend the local philharmonic series.

Take mini vacations without the children.

The Lord and His disciples knew what it was like to be busy. They were constantly on the go, serving and ministering to others. Knowing that relationships are not built on busyness, Jesus selected specific times when He could be alone with the disciples. Mark records one such incident, "And the apostles gathered together with Jesus; and they reported to Him all that they had done and taught. And He said to them, 'Come away by yourselves to a lonely place and rest a while.' (For there were many people coming and going, and they did not even have time to eat.) And they went away in the boat to a lonely place by themselves" (Mark 6:30–32).

There are times when it is essential to get away from the multitudes. You and your spouse need to go to a lonely place where you can revitalize your marriage.

This also means that you get away from your children. Again the Lord sets the example of leaving nine of the disciples, so that He could spend more time concentrating on the other three, "And six days later Jesus took with Him Peter and James and John his brother, and brought them up to a high mountain by themselves" (Matt. 17:1).

Some mothers have difficulty leaving their young children with someone else. But it is essential to go away for an overnight or weekend with one another and leave the rest of the family behind.

My wife and I love to go to the coast about three times a year for some rest and relaxation. We have gone on one-day jaunts as well as an extended two- or three-day period.

What about baby-sitting? How can you work that out? One way to keep down the expense is to swap baby-sitting responsibilities. Make arrangements with another couple to baby-sit their children for a weekend. Then allow them to return the favor when you go away.

Such weekend excursions should be planned well in advance,

and I guarantee that the benefits will be worth the invested time and effort.

Set aside time every day for each other for improving your relationship.

Daily communication will lay the foundation upon which to build a solid, healthy relationship. Everyone living in Fresno recognizes the need to water his lawn every day during the summer. One day without water will not kill a lawn, but withhold water for several days, and you'll turn a beautiful green lawn into a barren clump of dirt. Likewise, when you water your marriage with words of love, encouragement, and humor, that marital union will never dry up. Instead, it will prepare that relationship to become like fertile soil in which the seeds of faithfulness can be sown and produce a fruitful marriage.

Your time together may be at breakfast, or a telephone call during the day. It might be a periodic lunch, or a time of settling back and sharing the day's activities after the kids have gone to bed. It may include those quiet moments together when you pray with one another before you turn in for the night. Whatever time you choose, keep it as consistent as possible, interspersed with special times.

Finding time to be together is not an impossible task, but it needs to be given a high priority in your schedule on a daily, weekly, and special basis. It also should include those recreational periods.

What Should a Couple Do When They Are Together?

Now the question to be considered is what should couples do when they do make time for one another? In the beginning of Creation, God made woman for man and then brought her to man. The Scriptures explain, "And the Lord God fashioned into a woman the rib which He had taken from the man, and brought her to the man. And the man said, 'This is now bone of my bones, and flesh of my flesh; she shall be called Woman because she was taken out of Man.' For this cause a man shall leave his father and his mother, and shall cleave to his wife; and they shall become one flesh" (Gen. 2:22–24).

One of God's major purposes in marriage is that two separate individuals, perhaps from different backgrounds and possessing unique abilities, with varied interests and personalities, blend into a one-flesh relationship. In other words, they learn to know each other through conversation, experiencing common problems, observing one another, working together, and by just being together.

Use your time to get to know one another.

You may feel that you know your spouse quite well, but try this little quiz and see how well you *really* know your spouse.

KNOWLEDGE TEST

1. *Give your spouse's suit/dress size.* _____
2. *What is your spouse's favorite food?* _____
3. *Name a common fear which your spouse has.* _____
4. *What is your spouse's favorite or least favorite animal?* _____
5. *What does your spouse like most about you?* _____
6. *What does your spouse wish you would change?* _____
7. *Rate your spouse's opinion of himself/herself* (*circle*).

1 Very Poor	2 3 Poor	4 5 6 Good	7 8 9 Very Good	10 Excellent

8. *What do you think is your spouse's great ambition in life?* _____

After you've taken this test, share the results with your spouse. You may want to take a little more time to get to know one another.

Perhaps now you are asking yourself, *How can I get to know*

*my spouse in specific ways? How can I become more sensitive
or more aware of his/her needs?* I want to suggest three strate-
gies briefly: observation, communication, and cooperation.

Observation. I have learned much about my wife by consciously observing how she responds to different situations;
how she handles stress, and how she relates to people. I've
attempted to be sensitive to her moods, though she certainly
is not a moody person. Yet there are those times when I've
gotten the wrong reading, or I've been insensitive to what
she was thinking or feeling. Accurate observation is an art
and requires a lot of practice.

The problem in many relationships is that we just don't
open our eyes to see the needs before us. I've counseled many
husbands and wives who thought their marriage was going
well, only to awaken one day and discover that their spouse
has left them for someone else. They never took the time to
see the first signs of a troubled marriage.

Communication. A second strategy to help you better understand your spouse is communication. Communication includes
both listening and talking. And yet, many people would rather
talk than listen. They are of the opinion that talking is communicating. However, you communicate only when the other person hears and understands the message you are trying to send.

What then should you share with your spouse so that he/
she can know you better? And what should you attempt to
draw out of your spouse for better understanding?

Begin with your partner's feelings. Do you know how your
spouse really feels about you? Are you aware how he/she feels
about decisions you've made; or the way you treat him/her;
or the values you express in the way you live? Are you aware
of your husband's/wife's concerns about your work or attitude?
This is a good place to start. Ask your spouse how he/she
feels on these issues.

*You can also share ideas and activities in which you are
involved.* Perhaps you've recently completed reading a book.

Why not share some insights from it? Or maybe you've come up with an idea that you want to bounce off someone's mind. Why not share that idea with your spouse and get further insight into the possibility of making the concept work?

Don't be timid about sharing your personal fears, anxieties, or apprehensions, which may be keeping you from some very important action you need to take. Furthermore, communicating the important events of the day could be a very uplifting experience for your spouse.

The early church did a lot of sharing. They shared their finances (Acts 4:32–35), their food (Acts 2:42), their words of encouragement (Heb. 3:13), their failures (James 5:16), their burdens (Gal. 6:2), and many other personal needs and experiences. If that is the model life of the larger family of God, it certainly should be no less for the smaller family unit.

Cooperation. Self-centeredness is one of the character flaws we've all inherited from Adam. Some of the best selling books promote it as a high value and objective toward which each of us should strive. We are told how to become number one, or how to pull our own strings.

I read recently about the two actresses on the popular Laverne and Shirley TV program. Apparently they had a difficult time getting along with one another because each wanted to be number one. Each was seeking her own interests at the expense of the other. They even counted the number of lines each had. And one of the actresses managed to get the two head writers fired because she felt she was getting short-changed.

When the same self-centeredness enters the marriage relationship, war is inevitable. What Paul wrote to the church at Philippi applies well to the husband/wife relationship, "Do nothing from selfishness or empty conceit, but with humility of mind let each of you regard one another as more important than himself; do not merely look out for your own personal interests, but also for the interests of others" (Phil. 2:3–4).

The only way to experience this kind of relationship is to commit yourself to the value of cooperation. Webster defines cooperation as "working together with others." Be willing to give as well as take. This includes making decisions, making love, managing the family finances, choosing where and how to spend vacations, rearing children and many other life experiences.

Cooperation could be summarized best by Jesus' famous words, "Therefore whatever you want others to do for you, do so for them, for this is the Law and the Prophets" (Matt. 7:12).

Get to know one another when you are together—but don't stop at that point. Proceed to use your time in establishing some personal and family goals.

Establish personal and family goals.

The Bible declares, "Without consultation, plans are frustrated, but with many counselors they succeed" (*see* Proverbs 11:14). And the best place to begin the counseling process is with the person who knows you better than anyone else—your spouse.

Several years ago I spent at least one morning each week in a local restaurant to study and write. On several occasions I'd keep running into this one couple. There was nothing in their appearance that made them unique, but there was something special about their behavior.

Usually you can tell how long a couple has been married by watching their behavior in a restaurant. If they are newlyweds, they sit and stare at one another or giggle a lot. They like to reach across the table and hold hands, totally oblivious of the people around them.

The typical couple who has been married for a lengthy period of time, however, usually stares at other people or at their food. And they seldom talk with each other. Often they just read the newspaper and ignore each other.

Well, this unique couple was middle-aged, but didn't respond to one another like middle-aged couples do so often. They actually smiled at one another, as though they enjoyed being together. I noticed something else which seemed unusual. Each had a pen and a tablet, which they used continuously. After observing this couple for several weeks in that same restaurant, I decided to investigate the strange phenomenon. So I introduced myself to them and asked, "Would you be willing to share with me what the two of you do during these morning breakfasts?" They willingly agreed to share themselves with me. Each of them had a list of personal and family goals, plus a TO DO list of the day's activities. Those morning sessions were planning sessions for the day and the week. Some of the goals were long-range and others were more immediate.

That experience encouraged me to set aside every Saturday morning, when my wife and I go out for breakfast. Sometimes we just sit and discuss the past week's activities. Other times we write down short- and long-range goals. I've found those mornings to be extremely beneficial for a better understanding of one another, and as an opportunity to determine where we are headed in our marriage, family, and careers.

In addition to getting to know each other better and establishing goals together, time with one another should be used also for discussion of difficulties.

Talk through problems.

Proverbs wisely counsels, "Anxiety in the heart of a man weighs it down, but a good word makes it glad" (12:25). One of the tragedies of many marriages is that when problems arise, they are not dealt with properly. Some couples try to ignore the problems and hope that they will eventually disappear. Others immediately look for a place to lay blame, and find the most convenient person to blame is their spouse. Other couples engage in shouting or pouting.

The value of spending a regular time together is that it

offers the opportunity to talk through the little problems before they become big issues. Time together is like a safety valve, which releases the pressure before it builds up. Those problems you share may be related to your work, yourself, or your family.

Work problems. A husband comes home uptight from the office, because of a clash with his boss, a fellow worker, or a business deal that just fell through. He needs to vent his emotions and thoughts. An understanding wife can allow him to release the bottled-up feelings; express his opinion about the problem, and then help him work through the emotional and mental fog to get a clear picture of the real issues. Once he is able to distinguish between fact and fiction, and between what he can and cannot change, he is ready to take decisive action.

Personal problems. These also need to be shared. Such problems may include self-doubt, anxiety, guilt, a difficult decision, or future direction. It may be the wife who feels that she has no life of her own or no close friends. Or perhaps it's a husband who is totally undisciplined in his job, his use of time, or his eating habits. It's not easy to share personal problems with many people, so it's natural to turn to the one who loves you most.

Family problems. This is the third type of problem. It may include a mother who is not able to get along with her daughter, or a father who doesn't understand his son. The problem may also be the husband or wife who has been hurt by a careless word from the spouse. This may result in a festering emotional sore, which eventually expels its poison into the relationship. When you do take time together, be willing to deal with all kinds of problems at every level.

Work on projects.

Togetherness is not just a time for problem-solving. It also can be used as an opportunity to plan and work on projects. One of the most common projects which many couples enjoy together is the remodeling of their home. The time spent together dreaming, planning, and shopping for materials and furniture can be an exhilarating experience if it's done properly.

Another project some couples enjoy working on together is to host or teach a home Bible study in their neighborhood. It gives them an outreach opportunity, but also benefits them in their spiritual and marital growth.

Some couples have started a business together as a result of taking time to be with one another, setting goals, and talking through problems. Their business becomes a major project to which each gives of himself. This type of project offers the advantage to be together more often, but needs to be monitored so that the business does not become the master that enslaves the couple and suffocates the dynamic in their relationship.

Rekindle the romance in your marriage.

One other option you have when you take time to be together is to rekindle the romance in your marriage. I mentioned previously that when a young couple is dating, or during those early years of marriage, romance flows easily. You don't have to work at it. It comes with the package of youth. However, as the years pass, and the eyes sag, the belly and hips bulge, the hair thins, and the skin wrinkles, romance has a tendency to fade.

Therefore, it is important to rekindle that romance. Go out on dates together. You may even want to try double-dating with your children and their boyfriend or girl friend. It's a good reminder of how it used to be and can be once again.

You may try writing notes to one another. As a husband, you might try buying a personal gift for your wife, even though it's neither her birthday nor a special occasion. Just do it to be thoughtful, as an expression of your appreciation that she is your wife. Or surprise her by making reservations for dinner and taking her out. Most women like surprises. They enjoy doing things on the spur of the moment once in a while.

As a wife, you may want to go out and buy something soft and eye appealing to wear for your husband during those rare times when no one else is home, or when all the kids have gone to camp.

Romance does not have to fade as age flowers. It too can blossom in later life.

Conclusion

What can you expect to happen in your relationship when you make time together a high priority? Time together will give you a new appreciation for one another. It acts as a support system during those periods when nothing seems to be going right. It provides the opportunity to express differences, to learn from each other, and to pray with each other.

Time together will offer an excellent model for your friends of your commitment to each other. It communicates to your children that their home life is one of deep security, basted with a lot of tender love.

If this type of relationship appeals to you, then accept it as a challenge. Be willing to pay the price, which is nothing more and nothing less than taking time to be together.

PART IV

MAKING TIME FOR YOUR FRIENDS

10

Taking Time to Make Friends

Introduction

Though most commercials on television drive me up a wall, every once in a while one comes along and touches my soft spot. One such commercial was sponsored by the phone company. A man comes home from work and notices that his wife is a little teary-eyed, so he asks if anything is wrong. She replies that everything is just fine. He pursues the conversation, and she informs him that their son called from school. Immediately the husband asks, "Is he all right?" She replies, "Oh, he's fine." The husband asks again, "Are you sure he's all right?" to which she replies, "I said he's fine."

Bewildered, the husband wonders aloud, "If everything is fine, then why did he call?" With tears filling her eyes, she says, "He just wanted to tell me that he loves me."

The commercial was done with such good taste that you hardly noticed it was an ad for the telephone company. The theme song of their commercials is also a catchy tune with a powerful message. It says, "Reach out, reach out, and touch someone."

That's how you make friends. Reaching out to others as God has reached out to you. Friends are fun, and they can also become a life-saving support system in time of need.

149

In this chapter, I want to explain why it is so important to make friends, and then investigate some of those barriers people erect, preventing them from reaching out and touching someone.

Why Is It Important to Make Friends?

God made us as social creatures: people who need people.

You may not be conscious of it, but everyone has a built-in need and desire to be a social person. You deeply desire to love and be loved, to be accepted by others, to belong. That desire is natural, because God put it there when you were born. Think back to the original Creation for a moment.

After God created everything, including man, He declared, ". . . It is not good for the man to be alone; I will make him a helper suitable for him." So the Lord God caused a deep sleep to fall upon the man, and he slept; then He took one of his ribs, and closed up the flesh at that place. And the Lord God fashioned into a woman the rib which He had taken from the man, and brought her to the man" (Gen. 2:18, 21–22).

God's design for man and woman was to develop an intimate relationship in which both would be transparent. The Bible continues, "And the man and his wife were both naked and were not ashamed" (Gen. 2:25). Not only was there a nakedness of body but also a nakedness of soul. Adam and Eve were able to open up their inner selves to one another without fear or shame. They had no masks to wear—no reason to disguise how they really felt toward one another.

However, after they had sinned against God, their immediate reaction was to hide from God, and to cover up, so that neither could see the other's vulnerability.

Today we have the need and desire to become transparent in our relationships with people, but we also feel the need to put on masks, to cover up our true feelings, to protect ourselves from allowing others to see where we are vulnerable.

The result of these conflicting desires is stress. Such tension can be removed only when we begin to develop a resource of casual and intimate friends. Without friends, this innate desire for companionship will only frustrate us.

Friendship produces many beneficial results.

Friends can enhance your well-being. Recent studies give evidence that family and friends can have a very positive influence on a person's well-being, such as resolving our mental anxieties and depressions; helping us avoid psychiatric symptoms; and even protecting against certain diseases like heart disease, cancer, cerebral vascular accidents, and circulatory disease (*Friends Can Be Good Medicine,* California Dept. of Mental Health, 1981, p. 4).

In his book *Why Am I Afraid to Tell You Who I Am?,* John Powell refers to Dr. Harry Stack Sullivan, an eminent psychiatrist of interpersonal relationships. Dr. Sullivan has concluded that all personal growth, all personal damage and regression, as well as all personal healing and growth, come through our relationships with others. Powell elaborates:

> . . . There is a persistent, if uninformed, suspicion in most of us that we can solve our own problems and be the masters of our own ships of life, but the fact of the matter is that by ourselves we can be consumed by our problems and suffer shipwreck. What I am, at any given moment in the process of my becoming a person, will be determined by my relationships with those who love me or refuse to love me, with those whom I love or refuse to love (p. 43).

Research has also discovered that married people suffer less illness than single people. They also have fewer accidents than those living alone. And a nine-year study of seven thousand people in Alameda County, California, showed that people

with few ties to others had two to five times the death rate
of those who had more ties (*Mental Health,* p. 48).

In his book entitled *Stress and the Bottom Line,* Dr.
E. M. Gherman agrees with the principle that friends are good
medicine. He writes:

> People who are functioning members of their community, who
> are "socially healthy," also tend to have a higher degree of psycho-
> logical health and physical well-being. Those people who have
> developed a source of social support, who have close friendships,
> strong family ties, and warm relationships with neighbors and
> fellow workers, generally deal more effectively with stressful events
> than those who are socially isolated.

Friends can enhance your well-being. And they can also
encourage you in your spiritual development, our next topic.

Friends can encourage you in your spiritual development. The
New Testament provides ample examples of how friends encourage spiritual growth. When Jesus sent the disciples on
various missions, He always sent them two by two. Furthermore, the apostle Paul seldom traveled alone. He made his
first missionary journey with Barnabas and John Mark. And
when he traveled on his second and third journeys, he was
accompanied by several men including Silas, Timothy, Luke,
and others.

The New Testament also contains ways in which this growth
is to be carried out by the various members of the body of
Christ. We are to be devoted to one another in brotherly love
(Rom. 12:10); give preference to one another in honor (12:10);
pursue the things which make for the building up of one another (14:19); admonish one another (15:14); serve one another
(Gal. 5:13); bear with one another (Col. 3:13); comfort one
another (1 Thess. 4:18); and encourage one another (5:11).

The Bible also informs believers to select their friends carefully, for your friends can influence you for either good or
bad. Recall that Proverbs states, "He who walks with wise
men will be wise, but the companion of fools will suffer harm"

(13:20). Friends can be a great encouragement to help you develop in your spiritual life—if you've chosen friends who also have a personal and growing relationship with God.

Friends can help you develop self-discipline. It seems that we never need help to do those things that aren't good for us, such as eat too much, waste time, spend money foolishly, and become lazy. We *do* need help when it comes to disciplining ourselves to do those things that are good for us, like exercise, diet, manage money wisely, and pursue our work with a quality of excellence. If you find it difficult to develop a routine of self-discipline, call a friend and ask him to join you.

Friends can facilitate your success in life. You can make plans with a friend, work with a friend, be helped by a friend when you are down physically, emotionally, or spiritually. You can receive warmth from a friend's words or touch, and you can solve many of life's problems with a friend. Each of these benefits is identified in the Book of Ecclesiastes. Solomon ponders the values of friendship as he writes:

> Two are better than one, because they have a good return for their labor. For if either of them fails, the one will lift up his companion. But woe to the one who falls when there is not another to lift him up. Furthermore, if two lie down together, they keep warm, but how can one be warm alone? And if one can overpower him who is alone, two can resist him. A cord of three strands is not quickly torn apart.
>
> Ecclesiastes 4:9–12

When the chemistry of two or more people harmonizes, a dynamic relationship emerges which is difficult to quench. Each person seems to bring out the best qualities of the other. In his Proverbs, Solomon concisely teaches, "Iron sharpens iron, so one man sharpens another" (27:17).

And then, in addition to the value of enhancing your well-being, encouraging your spiritual growth, helping your self-discipline, and facilitating your success in life, friends also can aid you in your quest for self-identity.

Friends can aid you to know yourself. Most of us don't know ourselves as we should. We hurt people's feelings at times out of total ignorance, because we don't know how we are coming across to others. It could be the tone of our voice, our body language, something we've said or failed to say that triggers a negative reaction from others. Our intention was not to hurt, but we hurt people in spite of our intentions.

A friend can bring these flaws to our attention in an appropriate manner and at the proper time. In this way, our friend becomes a mirror, so that we can see our true reflection. On the other hand, the person who claims to be a friend and lets you stumble through life hurting people (and later being disliked by people) is not a genuine friend at all. To say, "I like him too much to let him know how people are reacting to him" is just spouting a lot of double-talk. When we see our friends in trouble, we go to their aid. And when they see us in the same predicament, they respond in like manner. A friend can help you know yourself also, as you open yourself to him. John Powell addresses this point when he writes:

> I have to be free and able to say my thoughts to you, to tell you about my judgments and values, to expose to you my fears and frustrations, to admit to you my failures and shames, to share my triumphs, before I can really be sure what it is that I am and can become. I must be able to tell you who I am before I can know who I am. And I must know who I am before I can act truly, that is, in accordance with my true self
> *Why Am I Afraid to Tell You Who I Am?* (p. 44).

It is important to develop friendships and relationships, because God made us social creatures, and because friendship, by its very nature, offers tremendous benefits. There is a third reason why friends are important.

There are many lonely people all around you.

In his book, entitled *Loneliness: The Fear of Love,* Ira J. Tanner states that "Loneliness is the single experience most common to all of us, yet is also the most misunderstood"

(p. xi). Another author, Harvey H. Potthoff, describes loneliness by saying, "At the heart of the experience of loneliness is the sense of isolation and separation. It may include the sense of being left out, of being rejected, of being estranged, of not being understood, of being abandoned. Loneliness involves the FEELING that there is no one and no thing responsive to our deep hunger for support and caring" (*Loneliness: Understanding and Dealing with It,* p. 14).

Who are these lonely people who need a friend? Certainly the *teenager* who is going through a host of changes. They are experiencing changes in their bodies. They change schools. They are moving into the adult world with all of its pressures. They are changing from dependence to independence. They wrestle between wanting their freedom but also craving the security of the family. They move among their peers who may be taller, more attractive, better skilled, smarter, and more socially accepted than they themselves. Teenagers may feel very isolated, confused, and even rejected as they move through these turbulent years.

The *single person* will feel lonely as he or she mixes in a society where marriage and family are looked upon as the norm, and singleness is viewed with suspicion or pity. In her book *So You're Single,* Margaret Clarkson reflects, "Most of us feel a need to belong—if not supremely to one person, then at least to a group where we are welcomed and esteemed and can find fellowship." She continues, "Friendships cannot be over-emphasized in the single life. They should be many and varied, always growing in depth, always increasing in number . . . while some friendships will be closer than others, few, if any, should be exclusive . . ." (pp. 84–85).

The single person who has never married, or the separated, divorced or widowed, all fall into this category. However, those who were once married, and one day awaken to the fact that they are single again, need special friends who can help them through the trauma of loss and their adjustment to the single life.

Then there are those who seem to have it all—the *leaders.*

You would never think of a leader who seems to have the popularity, the prestige, and the power to feel lonely, would you? But as one president after another soon admits, the presidency of the United States of America is probably the most lonely position one could have. And when he has to make decisions which could affect the entire history and existence of man, he stands alone. He will consult his most trusted friends, but the decision is his alone to make.

In his book, *Loneliness Is Not Forever,* James L. Johnson reflects on the loneliness of leaders, writing, "Mountain climbers say it often, 'The higher up you go, the lonelier it gets.' The same experience applies to leaders who, in their climb to the top, have found that the oxygen gets thin, the available companionship increasingly sparse. The plains and mountains and valleys of human intercourse, where a man or woman must maintain some vestige of the general, can provide territory for acute isolation and loneliness" (p. 122).

Is it really important to develop friendships with people? Without a doubt, for the following three reasons: God created us as social creatures who need other people; friends provide innumerable benefits; and there are many lonely people.

What Interferes with Our Making Friends?

In spite of seeing these great values of friendships, we all have a tendency to hold back. We impose on ourselves a sentence of self-isolation by the way we respond to the opportunities to make friends. Why don't we quickly run out and begin to make friends? What are those barriers which we erect for self-protection and self-preservation?

Let's begin with the various types of fears.

Fear of rejection. One of the most emotionally painful experiences one has is actual or perceived rejection. Everyone wants to belong and to be liked, but there's always a risk in being open and honest with others. And many have gotten burnt. One girl expressed this fear with these words, "I am afraid to tell you who I am, because, if I tell you who I am, you may not like who I am, and it's all that I have" (Powell, *Why Am I Afraid to Tell You Who I Am?*). Sometimes we keep people at a distance because we are afraid of what we don't know.

Fear of the unknown. We don't know what the friendship will cost us. We all have certain uses for how we want to spend our time. If we allow ourselves to get involved in the life of another person, it may cost us our time, our plans, our money, and perhaps even our reputation. The remedy for fear is given in 1 John 4:18, ". . . perfect love casts out fear. . . ." The one who loves deeply is more concerned about the need than he is the cost.

When Jesus invested time in the lives of others, He paid dearly. Many misunderstood His intentions. Others accused Him unjustly. It cost Him His reputation—and eventually His life. But His investment of time in the lives of other people has paid handsome dividends over the past twenty centuries.

Another barrier is our temperament.

Some people are born as social creatures, while others tend to be loners and self-sufficient. Both types of personalities have their special set of problems. The outgoing individual, who always wants to be with others and enjoys having a lot of friends around him, may also make many compromises in order to hold on to his friends. And the loner, who doesn't feel the need for a lot of friends, may isolate himself to the point where he never develops any social skills, and eventually experiences utter loneliness and rejection. Be careful not to hide behind your personality and say, "That's just the way I am." Whether you are more of an extrovert or introvert, you need to develop friends in whom you can confide, and whom you are willing to encourage.

Another barrier to good relationships is wrong thinking.

There are those who seldom want to socialize. They consider it a waste of time. I admit that some socializing can be a waste of time, but it can also be a tremendous investment of your time. I've found that if I go to a social event just because it's the thing to do, I usually receive little benefit from it. However, when I attend a special gathering with the intention of getting better acquainted or encouraging someone who is experiencing difficulty or some other such purpose, then my time is well spent. I've found that attitude and a little planning can reap some great benefits.

Another kind of wrong thinking is to expect friendships *just to happen.* People go around looking for that perfect friend, but when he or she doesn't appear, the person becomes frustrated. Friendships don't jump out at you. They must be developed. That takes time to be together, to talk, to play, to probe, to test the waters of trust, to laugh and cry together, and to experience difficulties together.

Another hindrance to developing deep relationships is shyness.

Dr. Philip G. Zimbardo, professor of psychology at Stanford University, surveyed 5,000 high school and college students and found that 40 percent of the people questioned considered themselves shy. On a national scale, that's approximately 85 million Americans. One in every 10 admitted to being "extremely shy" (*Why Am I Shy?* Norman B. Rohrer and S. Philip Sutherland, p. 7).

Many times we are not aware of shy people, because they come across to us as strong and in complete control. Barbara Walters, former hostess of NBC's "The Today Show" comments on this paradox. She says, "I have a slight inferiority complex still. I go into a room and have to talk myself into going up to people . . . I can't take a vacation alone, eat in a restaurant alone . . . I'm always hurt if someone says, 'She's aggressive. . . .' If I'm the epitome of a woman who is always confident and in control, don't ever believe it of anyone" (Rohrer and Sutherland, p. 39).

God provides His Holy Spirit to help those who are shy. Paul writes, "For God has not given us a spirit of timidity, but of power and love and discipline" (2 Tim. 1:7). The shy person often wants friends. In fact, he craves them, but is too shy to make the effort to contact a potential friend.

The emotional cost is another reason people don't develop lasting relationships.

When life treats you well, you and your friends enjoy the fruits of that relationship. But how do you react when a close friend informs you that her husband has just left her; or that her husband has just lost his job; or her teenage daughter has just run away from home? Suddenly your friend's problem has become your problem. Though you are saddened by the tragedy in that family, you are more than willing to help them endure the pain. . . .

Now several months have passed and your friend has gained no victory over the crisis. The calls become more frequent. You have a difficult time sleeping at night, because your friend is hurting so badly. You begin to feel guilty that you haven't experienced a recent tragedy. You are becoming weary, emotionally and physically drained. You don't want to refuse a friend in need, but you've run out of energy and wisdom as to how to counsel your friend.

Though some friends may become overly dependent upon you, don't take that as a signal to withdraw from people. Rather, handle that specific problem with love and firmness.

In *Today's Christian Woman* (Fall 1982), Ruth Senter gives

advice on how to identify and cope with the dependent friend.
She counsels:

> . . . The symptoms of an overly dependent friend are hard to
> miss. For example, if in a friendship I give all the advice, do all
> the comforting, all the listening, all the caring, I can be pretty
> sure that I'm breeding dependence. If I cannot share as much of
> my pain with my friend as she shares with me, it won't be long
> until I feel the drag and friendship becomes a giant boulder around
> my neck.
>
> If the pain of my friend becomes my pain, her pressures, my
> pressures, her sleepless nights, my wakefulness, then I may be
> carrying more of the weight than God ever intended in His com-
> mand to "bear one another's burdens." If her needs become the
> barometer of my life, continually demanding my time and atten-
> tion, diverting my efficiency, competing and winning out over my
> family and home, I may be giving—in the name of service and
> sacrifice—unhealthy doses of myself. Unhealthy doses for both
> my friend and for me. . . . Ironically enough, sometimes the kind-
> est thing I can do for a friend is to say no to her.

**Another barrier which may prevent us from seeking friends
is the problem of distrust.**

Distrust is usually the result of getting hurt in a former
relationship. You may have shared some intimate information,
which did not stop with your friend. Instead, that confidential
information was passed along from one person to another,
until it finally returned to you. You feel betrayed, used. It's
as if a part of you had been prostituted, dragged through the
streets, and returned in an impure form. So you make a decision
not to trust anyone again. You promise yourself that you'll
never allow anyone to see inside you. You build a wall of
protection around you and look at people with suspicion, questioning their motives, keeping them at arm's length.

In the meantime, you begin to experience a sense of growing
loneliness. You wonder if anyone really cares how you feel.
You would like to share yourself, but are afraid to trust anyone
again.

Living in an imperfect world, each of us will experience times when our friends will let us down. However, that's no reason to isolate yourself from everyone. Your greatest need is to expand your group of friends, and select carefully those who you feel more confident in trusting. *You need friends.* And the risks are worth the investment.

So whether you withhold yourself from making friends because of fear, temperament, wrong thinking, shyness, the emotional cost, or distrust, none of these barriers are worth that decision. *You need people and people need you.*

Conclusion

When you first started reading this chapter, you may have felt that you were the only lonely person around. Or perhaps you felt that you alone had been betrayed by a friend. Well, that simply is not true. Many have had similar feelings and experiences. That should not prevent you from developing good relationships with other people.

Why not put the past behind you and advance toward building new relationships with several potential friends? Your past rejections of God never stopped Him from His many attempts to establish contact and develop an intimate relationship with you. So why not do yourself and others a favor—reach out and touch someone today. Make it your goal to rearrange your schedule, so that you can make time for the establishing and building of friends.

11

How Can You Make Friends?

Introduction

How would you describe a friend? *Someone who is always there when you need him? One who is more interested in you than you are? A person who is not afraid to tell it like it is?*

The answer to this question is very subjective, but research has shown that men and women do not necessarily look at friendship the same way. According to British sociologist Marion Crawford, middle-aged men and women define friendship very differently. "By an overwhelming margin, women talked about trust and confidentiality, while men described a friend as 'someone to go out with' or 'someone whose company I enjoy.' For the most part, men's friendships revolve around *activities* while women's revolve around *sharing*" (*The Friendship Factor,* Alan Loy McGinnis, p. 11).

So perhaps our perception of a friend may vary on the basis of whether we are male or female, but it also may vary on the basis of what level of friendship you are working. This chapter will identify five basic levels of friendship, five essential qualities of friendship, and then conclude with how you can make friends.

What Are the Basic Levels of Friendship?

Studies have been made on how children understand friendship, and researchers have concluded that they operate on one of five levels. Let's describe each level and then demonstrate how adults often operate on these same levels.

The momentary playmateship (ages 3–7).

The child at this level does not distinguish between his viewpoint and those of others. Friends are valued for their material and physical attributes and defined by proximity. A child may say, "He is my friend because he has a brand-new wagon."

Adults may smile at such a childish view toward other people, but some adults never grow out of that perception themselves. Why do some adults make friends today? The same reason—because of the material or physical attributes of the individual. Consider how money attracts so-called friends.

Wealth. The writer of Proverbs observed, "Wealth adds many friends, but a poor man is separated from his friend" (19:4). This fact was borne out in the story of the prodigal who wasted his inheritance with loose living. He had more friends than he could afford—while the money supply was abundant. When it was all spent, his friends disappeared. He was left to himself. None of his friends took him in. No one would care for him. He was fortunate enough to get a job feeding the swine. It wasn't until he hit rock bottom that he came to his senses and returned home where he belonged, to one who was a true friend—his father.

James warned against building relationships with others on the basis of their wealth. He wrote:

My brethren, do not hold your faith in our glorious Lord Jesus Christ with an attitude of personal favoritism. For if a man comes into your assembly with a gold ring and dressed in fine clothes, and there also comes in a poor man in dirty clothes, and you pay special attention to one who is wearing the fine clothes, and say, "You sit here in a good place," and you say to the poor man, "You stand over there, or sit down by my footstool"; have you not made distinctions among yourselves, and become judges with evil motives?

James 2:1–4

Such friendships will be very shallow and last only as long as the money. Money, however, is not the only basis for a level-one friendship. There is also the position a person holds, which may attract friends.

Position.   Many who are in the high positions of an organization recognize that they will attract people because of their place in that organization. However, what they often fail to realize is that such friendships seldom run deep. You may earn people's respect (or even their envy) because you've reached the top, but you will not develop a deepening relationship if that person is primarily motivated to be your friend because of position.

Along with wealth and position you could add *popularity* as a dangling carrot.

Popularity.   Everyone wants either to be a winner or to be seen with winners. When a person becomes popular because of his or her athletic ability, brilliant mind, or some great achievement, he will collect around himself a group of people who call him their "friend." But again, you are a friend only as long as you remain popular. Sadly, one way some people have learned about their true friends is to see how people treat them after they've lost the money, the position, or the popularity.

One-way assistance (ages 4–9).

This is a second level of friendship. At this level, the child is beginning to distinguish between his perspective and another's view. However, he has not yet learned about a give-and-take relationship. His friendship is still based on everything going his way. A six-year-old girl may say, "She's my friend, because she does what I want her to do."

Today many adults are experiencing one-way friendships. Usually when this happens, the friends include a dominant and a compliant individual. The one controls the friendship, while the other does whatever is required to keep the friendship intact. The dominant friend enjoys his position of control and manipulates his friend to do whatever he wishes. The compliant friend experiences frustration at times, because he feels that his friend is taking advantage of him. However, the security of having a friend locks him into his compliant role.

Two-way fair-weather cooperation (ages 6–12).

This is the third level of friendship. At this level, friendships are based on both parties helping each other achieve self-interests. A child in this category would say, "We are friends. We do things for each other."

On the adult level, this is the kind of friendship you'll see in politics. "I'll scratch your back if you'll scratch mine." Compromise provides the balance.

This same attitude is often carried over into a marriage relationship. It's referred to as a fifty/fifty marriage. The marriage is good as long as each partner holds up his/her end of the load, but if one of the spouses fails to do his/her share, the marriage becomes strained, and possibly even terminates.

Intimate, mutually shared relationship (ages 9–16).

This is the fourth level. At this stage the child is preparing to enter the teen years. He moves from seeing friendship as reciprocal cooperation for each person's self-interest, to seeing it as collaboration with others for mutual and common interests. It's the time when secrets, plans and agreements are shared with each other. It's also the period in one's life when he or she may develop an exclusive friend. "He's my best friend. We can tell each other things we can't tell anyone else." "We know how each other feels."

The problem with this type of friendship is twofold. It can become very possessive, and it can exclude other potential friends.

We all know teenagers who develop such friendships to the point that, if their friend happens to befriend others, jealousy arises. They may cry out, "I thought you were my friend. What are you doing talking to Sally?"

However, adults are not exempt from this type of relationship. There are individuals and couples who cling only to themselves. Two or three couples may develop such a binding relationship that no one is permitted into the inner circle. And if one of those couples or individuals happens to reach out to someone else for friendship, the fireworks begin to fly. Accusations of disloyalty and "two-timer" may be hurled against the person or couple who wants to expand the circle of friends.

Autonomous interdependent friendship (ages 12 and older).

This is the final level of friendship. At this stage, the child has become aware that people have many needs. In a good friendship, each partner gives strong emotional and psychological support to each other. However, he allows the friend to develop independent relationships. A person at this level might say, "He's a very good friend but not my *only* friend."

Adults *should* be operating at this level. They need to expand their circle of friends. Though they will select a few intimate friends, they will not be possessive of them. In fact, a true friend will encourage you to expand your circle of friends, because he is more interested in your well-being than his own security.

The apostle Paul found a very close friend in Barnabas. It was Barnabas who brought Paul into the inner circle of the disciples. As Paul continued to grow in his spiritual life and ministry, he expanded his friendships to include Silas, Timothy, Luke, Epaphroditus, Archippus, and others. Paul had intimate friends but not exclusive friends.

What is a friend? A friend is not someone to use or manipulate for your own ends. He is not someone who has something that you want, and so you befriend him for selfish reasons. No, a friend is another human being whom you want to be with, no matter what his status. He is someone with whom you feel free to share yourself. He is a person whom you would help at any cost to yourself.

Let's delve a little further into the subject. What kind of a person would qualify for such a noble relationship?

What Qualities Should One Seek in a Friend?

In an article in *Psychology Today* magazine ("The Ingredients of Good Friendship," October, 1979), a survey of friendship revealed how important certain qualities are in a friend. Here are the top five: (1) keep confidences (89 percent); (2) loyalty (88 percent); (3) warmth and affection (82 percent); (4) supportiveness (76 percent); and (5) frankness (75 percent).

Consider first the quality of keeping a confidence.

On this basis, there are few true friends in Washington, D.C. It seems that no matter what is being discussed, it immediately leaks to the news media for everyone in the country to debate.

This quality in itself will eliminate a lot of potential friends. Some people have never learned when to keep their mouths shut. They run around from person to person, or telephone to telephone, spreading the latest morsel of gossip.

The Scriptures are clear on the necessity of keeping confidences among friends. Listen to what Proverbs has to say on the matter: "He who goes about as a talebearer reveals secrets, but he who is trustworthy conceals a matter" (11:13).

"A perverse man spreads strife, and a slanderer separates intimate friends" (16:28). "He who covers a transgression seeks love, but he who repeats a matter separates intimate friends" (17:9). When a person shares something intimate with a friend, he is entrusting a part of himself to that friend. As John Powell wrote, "Whatever my secrets are, remember when I entrust them to you, they are part of me" (*Why Am I Afraid to Tell You Who I Am?*, p. 86).

Many friendships have been broken because one of the friends failed to keep a confidence. Sometimes that failure is intentional, and sometimes it's unintentional. If you have difficulty locking up information which was given you in confidence, you may follow the psalmist's example when he prayed, "Set a guard, O Lord, over my mouth; keep watch over the door of my lips" (Ps. 141:3).

I don't know whether you've ever played the game tic-a-lock as a child, but when I was a young boy, we'd tell each other secrets. Then the person who just received the secret information would have to perform a ritual, pretending to be locking his lips with a key. He'd say, "Tic-a-lock and throw away the key." That was his pledge to keep a secret. We all need friends who have that ability to tic-a-lock and throw away the key.

The second most sought after attribute of a friend is his loyalty.

Walter Winchell, the renowned columnist of some years ago, has been quoted as saying, "A friend is one who walks in when the rest of the world walks out." That's loyalty. It's that quality which none of the disciples manifested the night on which Jesus was betrayed. They all walked out on Him. Near the end of his life, the apostle Paul was feeling the isolation and loneliness of his imprisonment and sadly wrote, "At my first defense no one supported me, but all deserted me; may it not be counted against them" (2 Tim. 4:16).

The Scriptures are also filled with evidences of one friend's loyalty to another. Think for a moment about Jonathan's loyalty to David. You first read about their friendship in 1 Samuel 18:1, 3. "Now it came about when he had finished speaking to Saul, that the soul of Jonathan was knit to the soul of David, and Jonathan loved him as himself. . . . Then Jonathan made a covenant with David because he loved him as himself."

Later, as David faithfully served King Saul, the king became intensely jealous of David. Saul's hatred of David boiled so greatly that he determined to kill the young man. The next chapter not only reveals Saul's plot against David, but also delightfully uncovers Jonathan's undaunted loyalty for David. "Now Saul told Jonathan his son and all his servants to put David to death. But Jonathan, Saul's son, greatly delighted in David. So Jonathan told David, saying, 'Saul my father is seeking to put you to death. Now therefore, please be on guard in the morning, and stay in a secret place and hide yourself' " (1 Sam. 19:1–2).

Later Jonathan returned to the palace and pleaded with his father to spare David's life, "Then Jonathan spoke well of David to Saul his father, and said to him, 'Do not let the king sin against his servant David, since he has not sinned against you, and since his deeds have been very beneficial to you. For he took his life in his hand and struck the Philistine, and the Lord brought about a great deliverance for all Israel; you saw it and rejoiced. Why then will you sin against innocent blood, by putting David to death without a cause?' " (1 Sam. 19:4–5).

Jonathan's love for David caused him to put his reputation and life on the line. That's loyalty.

The Book of Proverbs has a way of taking a volume of truth and putting it into capsule form. Here's how it describes loyalty, "A man of many friends [indiscriminate friends] comes to ruin, but there is a friend who sticks closer than a brother" (18:24).

What qualities are you looking for in a friend? A good place to begin is to keep your eyes open for someone who can keep a confidence, and someone who is intensely loyal to you and who would be reciprocated by your loyalty to him. But there are still other qualities.

Let's examine the third characteristic of a good friend— warmth and affection.

Your friend need not give you physical warmth and affection, but he should be able to provide emotional warmth and affection. Who is that person who gives out those warm fuzzies to you? The valid compliments? Those encouragements? The fatherly (or motherly) advice to stick it out when you feel like giving up?

Barnabas was such a friend to John Mark. Young John Mark traveled with Paul and Barnabas on their first missionary journey. However, after the first leg of the journey, John Mark decided that he had had enough of the missionary life and returned home. Barnabas was heartbroken, and Paul was furious. Eventually the rest of the trip was made so successfully that Paul and Barnabas decided to make another trip. Barnabas wanted to take John Mark with them again, but Paul was insistent that he not go along because of his earlier display of disloyalty.

The debate became so heated that Paul and Barnabas mutually agreed to go their separate ways. Paul selected Silas to be with him, and Barnabas built into John Mark's life. By this time, Mark was probably at a very low level emotionally. He knew that he had blown it by leaving Paul and Barnabas in the lurch. He wasn't proud of what he had done and knew that he deserved Paul's anger and rejection. But Barnabas was not only Mark's relative, he was a loyal friend who saw a scared young man who desperately needed to experience an emotional love and encouragement. Barnabas gave it.

Did that change Mark's life? Did Barnabas' warmth and affection make this young man a better person? Listen to the words of the man who saw little potential in Mark. As he writes from prison, Paul requests from Timothy, "Only Luke is with me. Pick up Mark and bring him with you, for he is useful to me for service" (2 Tim. 4:11).

Is there someone you know who desperately needs your warmth and affection? A compliment or word of encouragement? If you know of someone like this, he or she could become a possible friend of yours.

The fourth quality to seek in a potential friend is one who is supportive—such a friend won't let you hang by yourself.

To support others is to bear them up or to aid them. The Bible teaches us "Bear one another's burdens . . ." (Gal. 6:2). In another passage, the apostle writes, "Now we who are strong ought to bear the weaknesses of those without strength and not just please ourselves" (Rom. 15:1).

I think of Abraham's friendship with Lot, when I consider this quality. Lot was living in Sodom at the time, and during an invasion by another army, Lot was carried off as a prisoner. When Abraham received word, he could have responded by saying, "Well, he deserves what he got. After all, it was Lot who chose the best piece of real estate for himself, leaving me with land that sheep have difficulty grazing on. I wouldn't be surprised that God is disciplining him for being so self-centered." He could have responded that way, but he didn't. Abraham was a friend to Lot, and so he supported Lot when he needed it most:

> And when Abram heard that his relative had been taken captive, he led out his trained men, born in his house, three hundred and eighteen, and went in pursuit as far as Dan. And he divided his forces against them by night, he and his servants, and defeated them, and pursued them as far as Hobah, which is north of Damascus. And he brought back all the goods, and also brought back his relative Lot with his possessions, and also the women, and the people.
>
> Genesis 14:14–16

When I was away at college, my first year got lonely at times. I can recall that when I really felt down and a little discouraged, the Lord seemed to always bring my friend Dewey McConaghey to visit me in Philadelphia. Whenever he was in town, this man who had discipled me for over a year and was responsible for my being at Philadelphia College of Bible to begin with, also visited me as a supporter and encourager. We spent a few hours talking and praying together, and then he would leave to drive back to Lancaster.

By the way, one of the names given to the Holy Spirit is the name Comforter, or from the Greek, *Paraclete.* He is One who comes to your aid; One who comes alongside of you when you're troubled. That's what a genuine friend will do. He will be supportive of you, defending you before others.

One further quality to be considered is that of frankness.

There are some people whom you'll never get close to because of their wall of defense. Any slight criticism, and immediately they either withdraw in hurt or attack in anger. With a friend, however, you can be frank, open and honest. Recently I had to write a letter to a friend and turn down an offer to be part of a project to which he is totally committed. That was difficult, but it was even more difficult to tell him why I turned down the opportunity to get involved with him on that particular project. I supported him, but not that particular project. I hope he received it as a loving but frank reply.

The Bible declares, "Oil and perfume make the heart glad, so a man's counsel is sweet to his friend" (Prov. 27:9). This does not imply that the counsel is always to the friend's liking, but he knows that his friend is counseling on the basis of what is best for him.

Sometimes such loving frankness must come in the form of a rebuke. If a friend is causing problems among others by his attitude or behavior, he needs to be confronted firmly and lovingly. Such an event occurred when Paul was forced to take action against Peter in public. Paul tells of the account when he writes to the believers in Galatia:

> But when Cephas [Peter] came to Antioch, I opposed him to his face, because he stood condemned. For prior to the coming of certain men from James, he used to eat with the Gentiles; but when they came, he began to withdraw and hold himself aloof, fearing the party of the circumcision. And the rest of the Jews joined him in hypocrisy, with the result that even Barnabas was carried away by their hypocrisy.
>
> Galatians 2:11–13

Could you imagine how difficult that decision was for Paul? He was the newcomer, and there he was challenging the actions of those who were reported to be the pillars of the faith. Sure it was difficult, but it needed to be done. A true friend is willing to be open and above board if the friendship is going to become significant.

So you've caught a glimpse of a friend—one who can keep confidences; one who is loyal to you, warm, and affectionate; supportive, and lovingly frank.

Now that you've identified the levels of friendship and the qualities of a friend, go one step further and learn how to make a friend.

How Can We Make Friends?

Before we look at the right ways to go about making friends, let's pause to observe how *not* to go about making friends.

How not to make friends.

I've observed many wrong ways to make friends, but let's highlight what seem to be the three most common mistakes.

The overanxious approach. There's a cartoon I've always enjoyed about two dogs. One is a large bulldog named Spike. And the other, a little Heinz-57 variety. The little dog is so

overanxious to be Spike's friend that he'll do anything Spike
tells him to do. It's one of those "level-two friendships." The
little dog jumps around with his tongue hanging out, ears
flopping, and a big grin on his face. He says, "You and me
is friends, ain't we Spike? Huh, Spike, huh!"

That's how some people are to potential friends. They "Huh,
Spike" them constantly. They become overanxious. And before
a relationship can be developed, they want immediate assurance
that they've found a friend.

Such people are usually very insecure and cling to anyone
who passes by and smiles at them. They need to realize that
they can have many friends, if they are a little patient and
allow the relationship to develop, rather than force the relationship. They need to pace themselves. Give potential friends
some breathing room. Allow seed to take. A farmer planting
corn would be unwise if he were to run out a week later and
dig up seed to see if it took root.

The wrong-motive approach. A second wrong approach is
to make friends for the wrong reasons. When a person seeks
to establish a relationship for the primary purpose of what
he can get out of it, rather than what he can give to it, he is
in for rough sailing. Such a relationship may get established,
but it will be difficult to maintain. And if the friend discovers
the real reason for being friendly, it will hurt him and the
relationship will probably soon cease to exist.

People who tend to develop friendship on this basis are
either very insecure and are looking for a strong personality
to support them, or they are very ambitious, and recognize
some value in using the person for their own ends.

The obnoxious approach. A third way to avoid making friends
is to be obnoxious. A person may want friendship from others
so desperately that he goes out of his way to be noticed. He
is noticed, but not as a potential friend. He is seen as someone
who is very obnoxious, and therefore to be ignored or left
out of the inner circle.

Sometimes the obnoxious individual comes across as the

clown or the practical joker. Like that old ad on television: two men are at a party talking with one another. Soon one of these obnoxious clowns comes along and in a loud voice says, "Hi, Harry, old boy. What's the matter? Are your dentures slipping?" That's not how you make friends! Turn your attention now to some very positive ways to establish and maintain a friendship.

How to make friends.

Make friendship a high priority.   As long as making friends remains low on your priority list, you'll never find the appropriate time to reach out and touch someone. There are just too many other matters that demand your attention. You may need to go back to the previous chapter and remind yourself about the importance of friendship. "Loving our neighbor as ourselves" ranked below only one other priority in God's priority system—and that was to love the Lord your God with all your heart, soul and might.

Be friendly to others.   Now at first this suggestion may seem too obvious to mention, but when you observe the number of unfriendly people in the world who want to love and be loved, the obvious is more of a mystery to them. It's even amazing how many people who claim to love the Lord can be so sour looking, insensitive to people, and unconcerned with how they treat others. Nobody wants to be friends with someone who is always critical or who attempts to bully others. No one enjoys being around those who are ill-mannered and uncouth.

Therefore, show yourself friendly to others. Go out of your way to welcome the stranger or the new kid in the class. Imagine yourself walking into a room full of strangers, and then answer the question, *How would I want those people to treat me?* Once you've answered that question, go and do likewise.

Look for common interests.   This begins to narrow your field for developing more intimate friends. Often friendships begin with people who have a lot in common with you, such as the same-aged children; attend the same church; come from the same geographical background; have a common friend; or enjoy the same hobbies or recreational activities. You can be friendly to everyone, but you'll share common interests with only a few.

Become sociable. The next step is to become more sociable than you are, if you are more of the loner type. A hermit may have a lot of interests that others share, but if he does not mix socially, he will never be able to discover these people who share his interests.

If you've made it a habit to consistently turn down invitations to fellowship with people who want to get to know you better, you'll be the loser. You'll be seen as someone who wants to be left alone, and eventually, those who would like to be your friend, out of sheer frustration, will comply to your request.

Be hospitable. The Scriptures encourage this approach to friendship many times (Rom. 12:13; Heb. 13:2; 1 Peter 4:9). This can take the form of opening your home for church groups; inviting some couples or singles to your home after church; or providing a place for guest speakers at church to lodge. Hospitality is going out of your way on behalf of someone else, in order that they may feel accepted. It is showing acts of love. Frederick B. Speakman once wrote a book entitled *Love Is Something You Do.* And this is exactly the kind of love which the New Testament describes. Love is not limited to that tingling sensation you get when you are with the opposite sex. It is action oriented. When the Lord spoke to His disciples about love, He did so in the form of command. *Love one another.* And though the feelings of warmth cannot be commanded, acts of showing love can.

In his book *The Friendship Factor,* Alan Loy McGinnis speaks about showing your love to another by eating together. He writes:

One of the best ways to deepen a friendship is by eating together. It is no accident that so many important encounters occurred between Jesus and His friends when they were at table. There is something almost sacramental about breaking bread with another. Have you ever noticed how difficult it is to have dinner with an enemy and remain enemies?

So if you want to change an enemy into a friend, try inviting the person to your home and, with your feet under the same table, talk out the problem. Or if you wish to promote stronger relationships with more people, invite someone different to lunch every week or offer to meet people for coffee before work (pp. 54–55).

And finally, be yourself. No one likes a phony. And most of us are poor actors, finding it difficult to act what we are not. God never intended for you to be anyone but yourself. He never intended or expected Peter to communicate with people on the same intellectual level as Paul. And you never hear of Paul reaping three thousand souls on one occasion and five thousand on another. Likewise, Peter would have found it difficult to stand before the Greek philosophers and debate polytheism.

Don't be afraid of allowing people to know you as you are. They'll respect you for your honesty.

Conclusion

Friendships are not difficult to establish, but they seldom just happen by themselves. Someone must take the initiative to make contact. If you play a passive or a hard-to-get role, you may be spending a lot of time alone. If you are willing to take a risk and reach out to someone, you'll have a greater possibility of finding some individuals you may hardly know today. You may become intimate friends with those with whom you can share anything, within the near future.

God designed you for friendship. You will experience many benefits from friendship. *Many people need your friendship.* So why not take the initiative today? Reach out. Reach out and make a friend.

12

Time for Restoring Broken Relationships

Introduction

You've heard the hymn, "O that will be glory for me." But have you heard the alternate version? "In heaven above with those we love, o that shall be glory. But on earth below with the saints we know, well, that's another story."

Apparently the problem of getting along with the saints we know has been a problem since the church was founded in the first century. Euodia and Syntyche, two ladies in the church at Philippi, were not getting along very well with one another (Phil. 4:2). And in Corinth, the church was split in various factions (1 Cor. 1:11–13). Even Paul and Barnabas had such a sharp disagreement between themselves that they parted company (Acts 15:39). When close friends are no longer seeing one another and may even refuse to speak to one another, no one wins.

What do the Scriptures say about broken friendships and relationships? Is it always wrong to break a relationship with someone else?

This chapter will focus on two specific questions: (1) How should we view a broken relationship? and (2) what causes broken relationships?

How Should You Look at Broken Relationships?

At first glance you may feel that all broken relationships are evil, and therefore need to be restored immediately—but this is not true.

Some relationships should be broken.

Both experience and Scripture are very clear that not all friendships are healthy. In fact, many present commitments should be evaluated and perhaps even broken.

Friendship with the world system. The world system is that secular, humanistic system which excludes God from its value system. It's the system that deifies man and mythologizes God. It's a system of relative and ever-changing values. John the apostle warned his readers, "Do not love the world, nor the things in the world. If any one loves the world, the love of the Father is not in him. For all that is in the world, the lust of the flesh, and the lust of the eyes and the boastful pride of life, is not from the Father, but is from the world" (1 John 2:15–16). James elicits the same judgment on friendship with the world when he writes, "You adulteresses, do you not know that friendship with the world is hostility toward God? Therefore, whoever wants to be a friend of the world makes himself an enemy of God" (James 4:4).

If you find yourself thinking, talking, and behaving like those who are outside of a personal relationship with God, your friendship may have been misdirected and needs to be severed. A second relationship to break is that strong bond between a child of God and those who encourage him to forsake his moral and spiritual values and practices.

Friendship with those wanting you to leave your spiritual roots. Teenagers face tremendous peer pressure these days. Some of their best friends may encourage them to get stoned, indulge in free love, or rebel against parental authority. If your friends don't persuade you during those teen years, they'll try again as you begin to climb the occupational ladder to success. You'll be pressured, coerced, and manipulated to relax your standards by some who call themselves your friends.

Peter was aware of that pressure two thousand years ago when he penned this caution:

> For the time already past is sufficient for you to have carried out the desire of the Gentiles, having pursued a course of sensuality, lusts, drunkenness, carousals, drinking parties and abominable idolatries. And in all this, they are surprised that you do not run with them into the same excess of dissipation, and they malign you; but they shall give account to Him who is ready to judge the living and the dead.
>
> 1 Peter 4:3–5

You should never be surprised at what some of your friends encourage you to do, especially if they come from an entirely different mind-set and value system. But at the same time, you should resist the enticement, even to the point of breaking the relationship. If you continue to hang on to such special friendships for security reasons, you'll only hurt yourself. Remember the wisdom from Proverbs, "He who walks with wise men will be wise, but the companion of fools will suffer harm" (13:20).

You may need to break off an unhealthy relationship with a boyfriend or girl friend. It may be a schoolmate or a fellow worker. It may even be a neighbor or a partner with whom you are in business. How can you determine when you've reached that point? You discover that you are the one making the moral and spiritual compromises.

Some relationships will never be restored, and you must face this.

Just as it takes two individuals to make friends in the first place, it takes two to restore a friendship. Sometimes divorce is the result of two consenting adults, but often one of the partners does everything possible to reconcile the differences. The spouse may plead, pray, and beg the partner to restore the relationship, but if that partner refuses, the relationship will remain broken.

In his book *Growing Through Divorce,* Jim Smoke correctly observes, "Counselors do not work one party miracles in marriage very often. It takes two people working on the problem. The battle is already lost if only one person assumes responsibility. . . . If one person refuses help, your chances are minimal that you will get your marriage back together" (p. 16).

As in marriage, so it is in friendships which have been broken. If one of the former friends either ignores the fact that a problem exists, or refuses to restore that relationship, the possibility of reconciliation is minimal.

However, though some relationships should be broken and others may not be restored, I believe that other broken relationships should and can be restored. Why? Because the essence of the Christian life is *reconciliation.*

Some relationships can and should be restored.

God has reconciled man to himself. In the beginning man had fellowship with God. Adam walked with God in the Garden and enjoyed His fellowship; but when Adam sinned against God, that fellowship was broken. Instead of inner peace, Adam experienced guilt and turmoil. Rather than wanting to be with God, Adam wanted to hide from God. Instead of enjoying God's company, Adam feared God's presence.

Jesus Christ solved man's problem when He came to this earth. His mission was to make it possible for man to be restored to God. Since God was holy, and because man violated that holiness, the only way for reconciliation to occur would be for someone to pay the death penalty for sin—someone who would be as holy as God and yet 100 percent man. That Someone, of course, was the Lord Himself. When Jesus was crucified as man's sin substitute, God's holiness was appeased. The penalty was administered on a sinless sacrifice (2 Cor. 5:21). It is now possible for man to come to God. However, the value of Jesus' death is applied only to those who recognize and accept Jesus' payment for their personal sins.

This value is described by Paul in the Book of Colossians: "And when you were dead in your transgressions and the uncircumcision of your flesh, He *made you alive* together with Him, *having forgiven* us all our transgressions, *having cancelled* out the certificate of debt consisting of decrees against us and which was hostile to us; and He has taken it out of the way, having nailed it to the cross" (Col. 2:13–14, *italics mine*).

You offend God every time you sin against Him with your lips, your attitudes or your actions. Each sin decrees one more judgment against you. It's like another nail in your spiritual coffin. However, when you turn from your sin and invite Jesus into your life as your *personal* Savior, these judgments are eliminated and recalled no more. You begin life all over again with a clean spiritual and moral slate. God grants to you eternal fellowship with Himself.

Now if fellowship with God is available through Jesus Christ, then fellowship with a former friend is also possible through Christ.

God expects man to reconcile himself to others. The word *reconcile* means "to change or exchange" (change from hostility to friendship). When the word refers to man's reconciliation to God, the Greek word *katallassō* is used. This word conveys the thought that man must be reconciled to God, for man was hostile to God, and not vice versa. So man needs to change in order to have fellowship with God.

But when the term refers to men who need to be reconciled to one another, the word *diallassō* is used. The significance here is that there is mutual hostility and therefore mutual change must occur if the fellowship is to be restored. This word is used in Matthew 5:23–24, "If therefore you are presenting your offering at the altar, and there remember that your brother has something against you, leave your offering there before the altar, and go your way; first be reconciled to your brother, and then come and present your offering."

Because Christ has made it possible for you to turn from your sins against God and experience His fellowship, so does He make it possible for you to turn from your anger, emotional hurt, or bitterness against a former friend, and experience that friendship once again.

Since Christ's love and forgiveness made it possible for you to return to God, so your love and forgiveness can accomplish the same results with a former friend.

And now with these three fundamental perspectives toward restoring friendships as a context, let's consider the causes of a broken relationship, and then in the next chapter, the ways to restore that relationship.

What Are the Causes of Broken Relationships?

Specific causes would be as numerous as the relationships themselves, but here are some of the more general reasons why some friendships cease.

One person takes advantage of the other.

No one wants to feel used or manipulated, but when a person uses friendship for some self-serving purpose, that relationship may begin to wane. The Old Testament relates the account of two brothers who were friends early in life. On two separate occasions, however, the younger brother took advantage of the older. Let's look at the two episodes and notice the results.

The two brothers are Jacob and Esau. Esau was the older of the two, and was an avid sportsman who enjoyed hunting. He loved the out-of-doors. He was like the macho man you see on TV ads, and was the favored son of his father, Isaac.

Jacob, on the other hand, was a peaceful man who enjoyed staying inside. He was Mama Rebekah's boy. If he were living today, his idea of roughing it would be to camp in a fairly plush cabin that had only a black and white TV.

According to Jewish tradition, the birthright and the father's blessing were to be given to the firstborn son. The birthright was a double portion of the father's property (Deut. 21:17). The blessing was whatever the father wanted to bestow on the son. Therefore, both the birthright and blessing belonged to Esau. However, Jacob cunningly took advantage of his brother and grabbed both for himself.

> And when Jacob had cooked stew, Esau came in from the field and he was famished; and Esau said to Jacob, "Please let me have a swallow of that red stuff there, for I am famished.". . . But Jacob said, "First sell me your birthright." And Esau said, "Behold, I am about to die; so of what use then is the birthright to me?" And Jacob said, "First swear to me"; so he swore to him, and sold his birthright to Jacob. Then Jacob gave Esau bread and lentil stew; and he ate and drank, and rose and went on his way. Thus Esau despised his birthright.
>
> Genesis 25:29–32

The next time Jacob took advantage of his brother was when Esau was out in the field, hunting for food for his father. Isaac, the father, had planned to impart his blessing to Esau after he ate. When Mama Rebekah heard about Isaac's plan, she developed a plan of her own, so that Jacob could receive the blessing instead of Esau. The plan worked, and old Isaac, who was almost blind, blessed the wrong son. He put his hand on Jacob rather than Esau and said: "Now may God give you of the dew of heaven, and of the fatness of the earth, and an abundance of grain and new wine; may peoples serve you, and nations bow down to you. Be master of your brothers, and may your mother's sons bow down to you. Cursed be those who curse you, and blessed be those who bless you" (Gen. 27:28–29).

Later Esau returned, proud of what he killed for his father.

He then prepared a delicious meal for old Isaac and brought it to him, asking to receive the blessing. When Isaac realized what had happened, he trembled violently. Esau, on the other hand, responded with despair, saying about his brother, " 'Is he not rightly named Jacob, for he has supplanted me these two times? He took away my birthright, and behold, now he has taken away my blessing . . .' " (Gen. 27:36). And the final result? "So Esau bore a grudge against Jacob because of the blessing with which his father had blessed him; and Esau said to himself, 'The days of mourning for my father are near; then I will kill my brother Jacob' " (v. 41).

What a terrible price to pay for greed—the anger of a former friend.

Today this same greed has broken business partnerships, marriages, and other such close relationships. Using friends for personal gain is not the only cause for breakups. Strong, differing opinions also play havoc in many relationships.

The two friends hold strong differing opinions.

Usually good friends can weather this problem. They agree to disagree. They respect the other person's opinions, even though they may disagree with them. However, there are those times when a differing opinion will result in a different course of action. If neither friend is willing to compromise, the relationship may terminate.

A case in point is the relationship between Paul and Barnabas. Both men loved the Lord. They served God together, prayed together, fellowshiped with one another, and supported each other. However, the issue of John Mark came up. "Should we take him on the next missionary trip, since he left us on the first one?" Barnabas was affirmative on the issue, but Paul was negative. As they discussed the issue, the debate grew hotter, and each man became more rigid in his opinion.

Listen to how Dr. Luke describes the results, "And there arose such a sharp disagreement that they separated from one another, and Barnabas took Mark with him and sailed away to Cyprus. But Paul chose Silas and departed, being committed by the brethren to the grace of the Lord" (Acts 15:39–40).

People often inquire, "Which of these men was right?" Such a question is based on the assumption that one was right and one was wrong. Most people would give Paul the benefit of the doubt because of his zeal for the Lord, his writings, and the fact that you hear little about Barnabas after this encounter. Of course, the reason why you hear of Paul rather than Barnabas from this point is because the writer of the Book of Acts traveled with Paul on the next two missionary journeys. Therefore, he recorded only what he himself was witnessing—the events in the life of Paul.

Others favor Barnabas because he seemed to be the compassionate one of the two. He saw one man's need and was willing to sacrifice adventure, popularity, and personal growth for the sake of one young man with potential.

Personally, I believe both of these men were right. They each had a different vision or burden. One saw the needs of the multitudes, while the other saw the needs of one individual. Paul was more of a preacher and teacher, while Barnabas was an encourager. Paul focused on the many tasks at hand, while Barnabas concerned himself with the one person whose potential was untapped.

Thus it is possible that two friends could sharply disagree on a decision and both be right. Or again, both could be wrong. The important issue here is not in the rightness or wrongness of an opinion, but how that opinion affects the relationship. It's the inability to compromise on a nonmoral issue that caused this separation.

Perhaps the best way to handle such an issue is to cease the intimate working relationship but still remain friends. The Scriptures do not provide enough information as to whether Paul and Barnabas remained casual friends. We only know that their working relationship ceased.

A third cause of a broken relationship is an unexpressed hurt.

This cause is perhaps one of the most difficult to deal with. One person unknowingly hurts his friend. An emotional barrier is immediately erected by the offended party. However, he never informs his friend of the hurt. Instead, he just gradually works out of the relationship and busies himself with other things. When his or her friend calls, the excuse is given, "I'm sorry, I'd really like to get together, but I'm really so busy right now. Let's try to get together later." But "later" never arrives. The weeks and months pass with no direct relationship with one another, and eventually the friendship starves to death, due to lack of communication.

This approach is often used by people who are very sensitive and don't like a confrontation. They feel that it is better for all parties that the friendship fades like an early-morning mist. The only problem with that theory is that the rejected friend feels left out of a relationship, senses that something is wrong, but never discovers the real issue.

How much better it would be for the friend who was offended to share his feelings with the offender! He would not have to make accusations against the person or question his intentions. He could say something such as, "You probably aren't aware of it, but something you said offended me. I'm not questioning your motives, but I do want to clear up the matter and let you know how I felt when I heard what you said." This approach allows your friend to know what he said, and how you felt. It uses the following biblical guidelines in Proverbs, "Like apples of gold in settings of silver is a word spoken in right circumstances. Like an earring of gold and an ornament of fine gold is a wise reprover to a listening ear" (25:11–12). Your friend needs to hear how you feel as a result of things that he says or does. And if he is a true friend, he will listen to your hurt, apologize for hurting you, and restore that friendship.

One friend achieves greater success than the other.

One further cause of broken relationships is achievement. One of the aspects that many friends hold in common is a similar level of achievement. Usually friends enjoy a similar educational background, economic status, academic ability, and athletic, or recreational interests. However, if one of the individuals receives a substantial financial advancement, or a job promotion, or some great honor, his friend may feel somewhat cheated and have difficulty becoming truly excited about his friend's promotion or achievement. He has not learned the secret of "rejoicing with those who rejoice." Instead he weeps because he has nothing to rejoice over. He becomes hurt and develops bitter feelings towards his friend, due to his friend's success. And the more of a competitor he is, the more difficult it is to get excited for his friend.

King Saul, the first king of Israel, found himself in such a situation; and yet, he had little reason to feel that way. Saul had the honor of being Israel's first king. He was taller than most men in his kingdom. He had an excellent, well-mannered son, Jonathan. And he lived under God's blessing.

However, Saul, though humble in the beginning of his reign, developed a very proud spirit. He enjoyed the adulation of the crowds, the power and the wealth which came with his office. Furthermore, on several occasions, he willfully disobeyed God's clear commandment (1 Sam. 13:13; 15:9–11).

Because of Saul's flagrant disobedience to God, the Lord removed His Spirit from Saul, and an evil spirit troubled Saul. His servants looked for someone who could play the harp and soothe Saul's troubled spirit. David became that man. Whenever David played, Saul would be refreshed and emotionally well, for the evil spirit would leave him. Saul and David therefore became close friends. The Scriptures describe the relationship: "Then David came to Saul and attended him, and Saul loved him greatly; and he became his armor bearer" (1 Sam. 16:21).

So the relationship was good. In fact, Saul later promoted David. "So David went out wherever Saul sent him, and prospered; and Saul set him over the men of war. And it was pleasing in the sight of all the people and also in the sight of Saul's servants" (1 Sam. 18:5). Saul was so impressed with David's performance that he promoted him to be in charge of his army.

However, notice the change of attitude. Up to the time before David killed Goliath, Saul loved and honored him. But after the victory over Goliath, the Philistine, Saul began to feel differently towards David. The Scriptures indicate the reason for the change, "And it happened as they were coming, when David returned from killing the Philistine, that the women came out of all the cities of Israel, singing and dancing, to meet King Saul, with tambourines, with joy and with musical instruments. And the women sang as they played and said, 'Saul has slain his thousands, and David his ten thousands' " (vv. 6–7).

Can you picture the scene with its emotionally charged atmosphere? Imagine King Saul riding tall on his mount, watching the women run out to greet him with song and dance. He smiles a condescending smile, but as the words penetrate his ears, his smile turns into an inquisitive look—and then to a frown. *It can't be! Am I hearing them correctly? Why they are honoring my servant David more than me!* The Bible explains Saul's true reaction. "Then Saul became very angry, for this saying displeased him; and he said, 'They have ascribed to David ten thousand, but to me they have ascribed thousands. Now what more can he have but the kingdom?' And Saul looked at David with suspicion from that day on" (vv. 8–9).

Had David done anything wrong? Had he violated a friend's confidence? Had he manipulated Saul for some self-serving purpose? Absolutely not. David was totally innocent. He was a faithful and obedient servant. The only thing he did to provoke Saul's wrath was to become successful to the point that people honored him more than they honored Saul. And though

Saul eventually attempted to kill David on several occasions, David was loyal to his king until Saul's death.

You may have experienced such circumstances if you befriended some younger persons or new employees at work, and helped them with their jobs. Over the months or years, you encouraged them and rejoiced with them in their successes, because you were still above them on the executive ladder. Then the day came when they advanced beyond you, getting that promotion you wanted, or breaking your sales record. How did you feel? Could you get excited for your friends? Or did their successes bring out the worst in you?

Conclusion

Many other reasons could probably be listed for the breakup of friendships, but these four are enough to cause us to take a look at ourselves and evaluate any broken or strained relationships.

	Yes	No
1. Do I ever take advantage of my friends (use them for my purposes)?		
2. Do I expect my friends to accept my opinion whenever we have a disagreement?		
3. Would I rather break a friendship than share my true feelings with a friend who has hurt me unknowingly?		
4. Do I find it difficult to get excited for my friends' successes, even if they advance beyond me?		
5. Does my strained or broken relationship with others dishonor God?		
6. Am I more inclined to wait for the other person to take the first step of mending a broken relationship?		

How do you rate yourself on this evaluation? Any one of these questions where you've answered *yes* should have a yellow flag in your mind. It is an indication of a relationship problem.

Why not bring this matter to the Lord right now and ask for His cleansing and healing of this problem? Remember the phrase in the Lord's prayer, "And forgive us our trespasses as we forgive those who trespass against us." Will you forgive?

13

How to Restore Broken Relationships

Introduction

What do fishing and friendship have in common? Among other things, fishing is a means by which to make friends; and second, both fishing and friendship will be successful to the extent that they maintain a continuous mending process. Consider first how fishing can be used to develop a friendship.

When I was six years old, I received one of the most prized possessions of my childhood years—my own fishing rod. It was a birthday gift from my grandfather, who was an avid fisherman. Though I had never been fishing before, I had an idea how to use the rod. So as my mother and grandfather chatted downstairs, I grabbed an old bucket and filled it with water. Then I carried the bucket upstairs to my bedroom, dropped in my line, and patiently waited for the fish to bite. Within minutes I fell asleep. About an hour later, I was awakened by my mother and grandfather who were practically rolling on the floor with laughter, as they saw this six-year-old, with one hand holding the fishing pole over a bucket of water, and the other hand holding a thumb in his mouth.

It was obvious to my grandfather that his grandson desperately needed an education on the basics of fishing. A week later we went on our first fishing venture, which initiated an intimate relationship between grandfather and his grandson, lasting for the next eleven years, until my grandfather's death.

We enjoyed many pleasant times together, sitting on the banks of the Conestoga Creek in Lancaster, Pennsylvania. The birds chirped, as the sun peered through the early morning mist of those Pennsylvania spring days. Sometimes we'd catch five or six fish apiece, while at other times we caught nothing but colds.

The real enjoyment of sport fishing comes from being with a friend—talking, listening, eating together, laughing a lot. Catching fish can be thrilling also, but it isn't essential to feel that your time was worthwhile. Just being with someone you enjoy makes it worthwhile. So fishing is an excellent way to make friends. But the other factor that fishing and friendship have in common is the material used for a continuous mending process.

For instance, in commercial fishing, success is not determined by the beautiful scenery or the terrific fellowship, but in the number of fish caught. Since a fisherman's livelihood is dependent on what he is able to bring home, he uses much of his spare time, keeping his equipment in good working condition. Of course, commercial fishermen don't use rods. They use nets. They keep these nets in top condition. The Greeks have a word for that maintenance process. They call it *katartizō*. The gospel writer Mark uses this word when he describes Jesus calling James and John to discipleship, "And going on a little farther, He saw James the son of Zebedee, and John his brother, who were also in the boat mending the nets" (Mark 1:19). The word *katartizō* translated "mending," is also translated "to repair," "to put in order," and "to restore to harmony." When the fisherman's net is torn, he will not be successful. He will continue to lose fish unless he repairs the torn net.

Likewise, when you allow a relationship and friendship to be torn apart, both you and your friend will be the losers. You will each lose the opportunity for those intimate conversations. Neither will enjoy the security that someone really cares or understands. Silence will replace those supportive words of encouragement during times of depression.

Therefore, it is imperative to discover how to mend those broken relationships; how to put everything back in order; and how to restore harmony between two former friends. You will benefit from that mended relationship and God will be pleased. David put it well when he wrote, "Behold how good and how pleasant it is for brothers to dwell together in unity!" (Ps. 133:1). But how can a broken relationship be mended? Consider the following principles, which are not conclusive, but rather a sample of workable guidelines for healing wounded relationships. A good place to begin is to determine the source of the trouble.

Determine the cause of the broken relationship.

This is the most logical place to start. It's where the mechanic begins before he repairs your car. This is your doctor's starting point when he says, "Open your mouth and say, 'Ah.' "

Reflect back on the last chapter for a moment if you are experiencing a broken relationship. Was this relationship broken because your friend took advantage of you? Or did you have a falling out over a difference in opinion? Perhaps you've been hurt by something your friend said about you or to you, and have decided not to inform him or her why you are hurt. Or maybe it's because either you or your friend has made a significant gain in money, position, or popularity over the other.

The natural tendency is to blame the other person, but maturity demands that you consider what you may have contributed to the demise of the relationship. You cannot change your friend, but you can change your attitude and behavior towards him. Then once you know why the friendship has been strained or broken, you can take the next step—be willing to risk rejection.

Take the initiative.

It's natural to hesitate taking the initiative. Sometimes people hesitate because their pride has been hurt, or because they feel totally innocent. But another reason is because they fear rejection. *What if my friend doesn't want to restore the relationship? I'd really feel foolish!* The Scriptures are clear concerning who should take action first, whether you have offended a brother or whether he has offended you.

When you are the offender. When you know that the guilt lies on your shoulder, there should be no question who needs to initiate the action. Your friend has a reason to be angry or hurt. If you've taken advantage of the friendship or slandered him in any way, go and apologize. Ask his forgiveness. Tell him that you want harmony restored in your relationship.

Jesus said: "If therefore you are presenting your offering at the altar, and there remember that your brother has something against you, leave your offering before the altar, and go your way; first be reconciled to your brother, and then come and present your offering" (Matt. 5:23–24). Likewise, the apostle John writes, "If someone says, 'I love God,' and hates his brother, he is a liar; for the one who does not love his brother whom he has seen, cannot love God whom he has not seen" (1 John 4:20).

If you claim to be a Christian and worship God each week, God is saying to you, "Why should I accept your worship of Me when you refuse to make things right with your friend? Get things straightened out between the two of you, then honor Me with a pure heart and clean hands."

Few people will argue the point. The offender should certainly initiate reconciliation between himself and the offended. But what about the offended's responsibility? Should he merely wait for the offender, or should he initiate action towards restoring that relationship also?

When you have been offended. A worldly perspective would encourage you to hold your ground and not budge until the offender apologizes to you—but the Scriptures counsel otherwise. The Bible says, "Let all bitterness and wrath and anger and clamor and slander be put away from you, along with all malice. And be kind to one another, tender-hearted, forgiving each other, just as God in Christ also has forgiven you" (Eph. 4:31–32). Now how did God forgive you?

First He took the initiative towards you. You offended Him, but God's love for you drove Him to offer you forgiveness, even though you were still hostile towards Him. John, the apostle, wrote, "We love, because He first loved us" (1 John 4:19). Therefore, even though you are the one who was hurt, or perhaps the innocent party, you have a responsibility of initiating reconciliation. It is here where your Christian faith will be most severely tested. If Christ can make a difference in a person's life, this is the place where it should show. And even at a time when you are willing to take the initiative, your offer may be rejected. Your friend may feel very guilty if he has offended you, and *you* offer the opportunity for reconciliation. His guilt may drive him to reject your offer, but at least you can have the satisfaction of a clear conscience, knowing that you did what you could to restore the broken relationship. You'll have experienced what God experiences every day when He offers forgiveness to those who have offended Him— rejection (Luke 17:25). A third step toward bringing harmony out of discord is to approach your former friend in the spirit of humbleness.

Approach your friend in humility.

The natural tendency is to approach the other person with a slate of offenses in our back pocket, in case he accuses us of wrongdoing. You may want to tell the person, "Look, I know that I've done some things wrong in our relationship, but they are nothing in comparison with what you did to me. So I'll forgive you for all those lousy things you did to me. And I expect you to forget about the way I reacted to you, even though you caused me to react that way."

No, that's not the way to bridge the gap! A humble attitude doesn't accuse. It rather seeks restoration. Consider that famous passage in Philippians which describes Jesus' humility. In it are found several characteristics of true humility: "Have this attitude in yourselves which was also in Christ Jesus, who, although He existed in the form of God, did not regard equality with God a thing to be grasped, but emptied Himself, taking the form of a bondservant, and being made in the likeness of men. And being found in appearance as a man, He humbled Himself by becoming obedient to the point of death, even death on a cross" (Phil. 2:5–8).

Among many other truths presented in this passage, at least three characteristics of humility are presented: (1) a refusal to demand one's rights; (2) a willingness to identify with the offender; and (3) a willingness to do what is essential to restore a relationship.

Humility gives up its rights. Today everyone wants their rights. Everyone wants to be treated equally, and if partiality is shown, the picket signs come out and the rallies begin. When the thought of restoring a broken relationship occurs, each party has a tendency to protect his or her rights.

Remember the account of Abraham and Lot. They decided that it was necessary to separate company, but not friendship, since their herds were so large. Abraham demonstrated humility by giving up his right to make the first choice. He could have chosen the best land for himself and given Lot the leftovers. Instead he told Lot, " '. . . Please let there be no strife between you and me, nor between my herdsmen and your herdsmen, for we are brothers. Is not the whole land before you? Please separate from me: if to the left, then I will go

to the right; and if to the right, then I will go to the left' "
(Gen. 13:8–9).

Abraham was secure enough in God to know that whatever
Lot's decision was really immaterial to Abraham's welfare.
God was going to provide for Abraham, whether Lot chose
to take the best or the least for himself.

Humility, therefore, is willing to risk one's rights for the
sake of harmony—but it goes a step further.

Humility identifies itself with the offender. Humility recognizes the nature of human nature. Everyone says and does
things for which he is later ashamed. Paul hit right on the
target when he asked the Roman believers this question regard-
ing former sins, "Therefore what benefit were you then deriving
from the things of which you are now ashamed? For the outcome of those things is death" (Rom. 6:21).

For some people, the outcome is the death of a reputation.
For others, the death of a relationship. Have you ever caught
yourself saying to yourself, *I wish I hadn't said that?*

So your friend offended you. He was wrong in what he
did, but your humble attitude will recognize that "all have
sinned and fall short of the glory of God" (Rom. 3:23), including yourself. Your friend needs your willingness to understand
him. I'm not suggesting that you give him a blank check,
but I do see humility extending its hand to the offender, in
spite of his fault.

Humility is willing to pay the price for harmony. A third
characteristic of humility is willingness to do whatever it takes
for harmony, within the guidelines of biblical truth. The Lord
was willing to conform Himself to a plan of action, which
He knew would lead to His eventual death; but He counted
this ultimate act of love a necessity, if harmony with mankind
were going to be made possible. Likewise, the truly humble
person will do whatever is necessary to mend a torn relationship.

In the last chapter you read how Jacob swindled Esau out

of his birthright and his father's blessing. You saw how enraged Esau became. And that rage became an obsession to Esau, as he vowed revenge on his brother Jacob. Do you know the rest of the story?

Years pass between Jacob's last cunning act and his next encounter with Esau. Jacob left his family when he heard of his brother Esau's vow for revenge. He traveled east, to where his Uncle Laban was living. During the next twenty years, Jacob accumulated a large family and great wealth. After this period, he decided to return to his home, but was apprehensive because of a twenty-year-old problem that had never been solved: the broken relationship with his brother, Esau. For twenty years they had not spoken to one another. They had not corresponded in any way. And now Jacob would have to pass through Esau's land in order to return home.

As Jacob ventured toward home, one of the messengers, whom Jacob had sent ahead to break the ice, returned saying, " 'We came to your brother Esau, and furthermore he is coming to meet you, and four hundred men are with him' " (Gen. 32:6). Jacob was beside himself wondering what to do. He finally decided to divide his company into two groups, expecting a possible invasion. Then he developed a plan of action, which he hoped would appease his brother's wrath. He determined to give Esau "two hundred female goats and twenty male goats, two hundred ewes and twenty rams, thirty milking camels and their colts, forty cows and ten bulls, twenty female donkeys and ten male donkeys" (Gen. 32:14–15).

So he selected the animals, brought them to his servants, and told them to deliver the animals to Esau. The servants were to arrange the livestock in groups. They would first deliver the goats; then the ewes and rams; next the camels and colts; followed by the cows and bulls; and finally the donkeys. The process would highlight Jacob's generosity to Esau, and demonstrate his willingness to heal old wounds by repaying Esau with what amounted to a birthright and blessing.

Did the plan work? Look at the Genesis record. Jacob came

to Esau bowing down to the ground seven times, until he came to his brother. "Then Esau ran to meet him and embraced him, and fell on his neck and kissed him, and they wept" (33:4). For Jacob, humility meant that he would do whatever was necessary to restore that twenty-year broken relationship. His price came in the form of restitution. Jacob cunningly took advantage of Esau; therefore, he knew that reconciliation would be possible only if he were willing to make restitution for what he had taken.

For some people today, that may be a price they'll have to pay to heal a broken relationship. Whatever they took from their friend should be returned in some form, to show evidence that they mean business.

Admit whatever you contributed to the cause or continuation of the broken relationship.

This is the fourth principle for mending what is torn. Two of the most difficult words in the English language for many people are the words *I'm sorry.* Each party is not necessarily equally guilty in causing a friendship to cease. One friend may want to continue the relationship, but at the time the other person turns down all attempts. The tendency at that point is to think, *All right. I've done everything I can think of to restore harmony between us, and he won't budge. So I'm placing the burden on his shoulders. If he ever changes his mind, he'll have to come back crawling.*

That's a common reaction, but not a wise one. A better attitude would be to let some time pass, and then approach your friend again. This time, however, admit that you feel badly for having allowed this broken relationship to continue so long. Inform your friend that you would like to get back together again. Perhaps you could ask, "What can I do to help us build a better relationship than we had before?" Don't give up just because you tried and it didn't work out earlier.

Allow time to heal the wounds.

Because of the emotional turmoil which follows the breakup of a close friendship, restoration is not so easy. The emotions run deep. A cooling-off period is essential for most emotional scars to be healed. Allow time for you and your friend to evaluate the real problem. Allow time for seeking wise counsel from other close friends. Allow time for God to do a work in both of your lives, dealing with your attitudes toward yourself and toward the other person. Allow time to get apart from the regular contact with one another, so that your emotions don't cloud your thinking. Though I wouldn't recommend the twenty years it took before Jacob and Esau could get back together, a time to develop a fresh perspective on that relationship is vital. Don't rush into restoration, but do work towards it. As Ecclesiastes 3:5, 7 puts it, there is "a time to throw stones, and a time to gather stones; a time to embrace, and a time to shun embracing . . . . A time to tear apart, and a time to sew together; a time to be silent, and a time to speak."

Use the help of a third party.

One of the broken relationships recorded in Scripture is found hidden away in one of the shortest books of the Bible—Philemon. Philemon was a wealthy businessman who owned many slaves, one of whom was Onesimus. After a period of serving Philemon, Onesimus ran away to Rome, and it is believed that he took some of Philemon's possessions with him. As far as Philemon was concerned, Onesimus was a good-for-nothing, runaway slave. If Philemon ever caught up to Onesimus, he could have put him to death. But being a mature Christian (who maintained an excellent reputation in the community), he would never consider taking such drastic measures. However, he had been offended by his servant's unfaithfulness.

Unknown to Philemon, Onesimus somehow meets the apostle Paul in a Roman prison. Whether he himself was thrown in jail, or just visited there, is unknown, but he did come across Paul, who led him into a personal relationship with Jesus Christ. As time passed, Paul built into the spiritual life of Onesimus, while Onesimus ministered to Paul in other ways. Later, however, both men knew that the broken relationship between Philemon and Onesimus had to be restored. Therefore, Paul intervened on behalf of Onesimus by writing a letter to Philemon and sending it by way of Onesimus. In that letter, Paul informed Philemon of the spiritual transformation which had taken place in Onesimus' life. He writes: "I appeal to you for my child, whom I have begotten in my imprisonment, Onesimus, who formerly was useless to you, but now is useful both to you and to me. And I have sent him back to you in person, that is, sending my very heart, whom I wished to keep with me, that in your behalf he might minister to me in my imprisonment for the gospel . . ." (Philemon 10–13).

The apostle continues to inform Philemon that Onesimus may have left him under the permissive will of God because of God's plans to change his life. He says, "For perhaps he was for this reason parted from you for a while, that you should have him back forever, no longer a slave, but more than a slave, a beloved brother, especially to me, but how much more to you, both in the flesh and in the Lord" (Philemon 15–16).

Then Paul asks Philemon to receive Onesimus back without punishment. "If then you regard me a partner, accept him as you would me. But if he has wronged you in any way, or owes you anything, charge that to my account" (vv. 17–18).

You may not have any broken friendships yourself; however, why not consider the possible role of mediator between two estranged friends? Many people need a third party who will be objective and have no emotional involvement in the relationship, other than a strong desire to see two old friends heal their differences and live in harmony with one another. Jesus said, " 'Blessed are the peacemakers, for they shall be called sons of God' " (Matt. 5:9).

On the other hand, if you are estranged from a former friend, why not consider asking a mutual friend to begin the work of reconciliation between the two of you?

Pray.

This final principle I need to share with you may sound trite, but it is given in all seriousness. When attempting to mend a torn relationship, by all means *pray*. In a very real sense, prayer is the act of calling in a third party to handle the dispute. "But what should I pray about?" you may ask. Pray for yourself and your former friend.

Pray for yourself. At first thought, you might want to pray about your former friend. You may want God to bring that friend to his senses—or you may hope that God gets even with him for what he did to you. But this isn't the place to begin. You cannot change your friend, but you can change *yourself.* So that's the place to begin. Consider the following elements in your prayer for yourself: honesty, clarity, confession, and wisdom.

(1) *Honesty.* Ask the Lord to help you to be brutally honest with yourself. It's easy to see your friend's problem, but are you without fault? Are your hands pure? Jesus tells it like it is when He asks: "And why do you look at the speck in your brother's eye, but do not notice the log that is in your own eye? Or how can you say to your brother, 'Let me take the speck out of your eye,' and behold, the log is in your own eye? You hypocrite, first take the log out of your own eye, and then you will see clearly enough to take the speck out of your brother's eye" (Matt. 7:3–5). Once a person can become honest with himself, he will begin to see things more clearly.

(2) *Clarity.* As one continues to pray and remove the logs from his eyes, he will gain a new perspective and develop a new attitude towards the friend and the problem.

Our vision is not only hindered by logs in our eyes, but also by our emotions. Bitterness, anger, fear, and frustration have a tendency to cloud the issue. To say, "This is how I see it. Therefore, that is how it is," does not exhibit wisdom. It rather demonstrates shallow thinking. Therefore, ask God to clarify the issue—to help you see your friend, the problem, and yourself with twenty/twenty vision. As you begin to see clearly, be willing to confess where you misjudged your friend.

(3) *Confession.* It is always easier to condemn than it is to confess. But condemnation is often a premature act. Once a person can see where he has contributed to the problem rather than to the solution, he has something to confess. Then once confession is made and forgiveness is received, seek God's intimate wisdom as to how you should approach your friend with a proposal to restore the relationship.

(4) *Wisdom.* You'll need wisdom as to what you should or should not say. You'll need wisdom for the proper time to approach your former friend. And where can you find wisdom? James gives the direction, "But if any of you lacks wisdom, let him ask of God, who gives to all men generously and without reproach, and it will be given him" (James 1:5).

God is the source of wisdom. However, when it comes to relating to other people, man has a tendency to draw wisdom out of another well, referred to in Scripture as the wisdom of the world (1 Cor. 1:21).

James contrasts both the qualities and the results of these two wisdom sources. Man's wisdom is characterized as coming from the world, and is earthly, natural, demonic; resulting in jealousy and selfish ambition, disorder and every evil thing (James 3:14–16). However, God's wisdom is characterized by being pure, peaceable, gentle, reasonable, full of mercy and good fruits, unwavering and without hypocrisy. The outcome of that wisdom is righteousness (vv. 17–18).

Therefore, the only way to unite what has been divided, is to seek and then to apply God's wisdom to the broken relationship. So ask God to supply you with a generous portion of His wisdom so you will know how you can make it easier for your friend to be restored.

Pray for yourself—that God would help you to be honest with yourself; gain clear insight into the problem; give you the courage to confess what needs confessing; and grant you His wisdom as you initiate the contact. But don't stop with yourself.

Pray for your friend.

The biblical and practical purpose of confrontation is not to punish, to ridicule or to belittle—but rather to restore, to heal, and to mend.

Nathan the prophet confronted David about his adultery for a single purpose—to restore David's fellowship with God. Paul confronted Peter publicly to restore the former fellowship which the believing Jews had with the believing Gentiles. Pray that God would give your friend the desire to be reconciled to you. Ask the Lord to help your friend be honest with himself; to see the issue clearly; to confess where he added to the problem; and to desire God's wisdom in resolving the problem.

Conclusion

These principles may not restore every broken relationship, but they can at least begin the process of bringing two alienated people into contact with one another.

Are you alienated from a former friend? Is that broken relationship helping or hindering your life? Is it honoring or dishonoring to God? Why not begin the restoration process today, so that you will eventually be able to enjoy the experience described in the psalm, "How good and how pleasant it is for brethren to dwell together in unity."

Are you alienated from God? Why not restore that relationship by confessing the fact that you have offended His holiness and righteousness. Now that you realize what sin really is, you want to come into eternal fellowship with Him. This is exactly what He is waiting to hear from you. He has said: "Behold, I stand at the door and knock; if any one hears My voice and opens the door, I will come in to him, and will dine with him, and he with Me" (Rev. 3:20).

He is knocking at your life's door. Will you open it right now for Him? Here is a suggested prayer, which you may want to pray:

Dear Jesus, Thank You for wanting to come into my life. I know that I don't deserve Your love, but I accept it anyway. I confess that I have sinned against You and I'm very sorry for every sin I've ever committed. Please forgive me. I ask You to come into my life and to stay there forever. Thank You for hearing my prayer and for making me a new person. I ask this in Your name, *amen.*

Part V

MAKING TIME FOR GOD

14

Man's Greatest Neglect of Time

Introduction

What is man's most neglected use of time? The few minutes he may spend with his family? The time he spends reading? No, there is a greater neglect than either of these.

A recent study reveals that an average 70-year-old man has spent 24 years sleeping; 14 years working; 8 years in amusement; 6 years at the dinnertable; 5 years in transportation; 4 years in conversation; 3 years in education; 2 years in studying and reading. His other 4 years were spent in miscellaneous pursuits, except for 45 minutes he spent on Sundays, and 5 minutes he devoted to prayer each day. This adds up to the tremendous total of 5 months that he gave to God over the 70-year span!

Time with God. That is man's most neglected use of his time. And to fill our lives with everything *but* God is very foolish.

Why Is It Foolish to Neglect Time with God?

Man's spiritual life alone is eternal.

Nothing else that man either possesses or works for will last forever. Everything else is subject to change and decay.

Man's body will die. Our bodies are not immortal. In fact, the Bible clearly declares that "flesh and blood cannot inherit the kingdom of God" (1 Cor. 15:50). God informed Adam of his mortality when He said, " 'By the sweat of your face you shall eat bread, till you return to the ground, because from it you were taken; for you are dust, and to dust you shall return' " (Gen. 3:19). It's not very flattering to realize that no matter how well you keep your diet, or how many vitamin supplements you inject, or how many miles you jog, you are dust and will eventually return to dust. Your body will not make it to heaven. Just as a fish cannot live out of water because its body was designed for living in the water, so our bodies cannot live in heaven, for they are designed for earth.

I go to a local health club several times a week. I enjoy keeping my body as fit as I can discipline myself to do. However, as I watch some of the young men spend hours each day, keeping their bodies conditioned, I often wonder how much time they are giving to develop the inner man that is going to live forever.

The apostle Paul informed Timothy, ". . . discipline yourself for the purpose of godliness; for bodily discipline is only of little profit, but godliness is profitable for all things, since it holds promise for the present life and also for the life to come" (1 Tim. 4:7–8).

Indeed, it is foolish to neglect God, since our inner self alone is going to live forever.

Man's money is temporal. Most people spend a lot of time trying to make money, because it provides a sense of security for them. The more they have, the more secure they think they will feel, but money is a weak basis for security. The writer of the Proverbs expresses this thought when he warns, "Do not weary yourself to gain wealth. Cease from your consideration of it. When you set your eyes on it, it is gone. For wealth certainly makes itself wings, like an eagle that flies toward the heavens" (23:4–5).

And not only is wealth transitory in the present life—it is also completely worthless in the future life. The New Testament verifies this fact by stating, "For we have brought nothing into the world, so we cannot take anything out of it either" (1 Timothy 6:7). When billionaire Howard Hughes died, he left all his wealth behind. Not a penny escaped to heaven.

Man's body will eventually die. His money provides no real security. And even his works will not last forever, except those works done for God's glory.

Man's works are limited.   The wisest king on earth concluded, after perusing over his great accomplishments on earth: "Thus I hated all the fruit of my labor for which I had labored under the sun, for I must leave it to the man who will come after me. And who knows whether he will be a wise man or a fool? Yet he will have control over all the fruit of my labor for which I have labored by acting wisely under the sun. This too is vanity. Therefore, I completely despaired of all the fruit of my labor for which I had labored under the sun" (Eccl. 2:18–20).

Think of all the men and women who qualify as workaholics. Their job possesses them. They live for work. They spend hour upon hour cranking out work. Yet, none of their labor will go beyond this earth, except for that which is done for God's glory. For those alone it will be said " '. . . Blessed are the dead who die in the Lord from now on!' " Yes, says the Spirit. " 'That they may rest from their labors, for their deeds follow with them' " (Rev. 14:13).

Man's fame is fleeting.   A fourth area in which man spends a lot of time, attempting to achieve, is fame. He wants to be first among his peers. To be the godfather of his own group, whether large or small. He seeks recognition—but even fame is fleeting. Many of the past presidents of the United States are known only by name, and yet they held one of the highest offices in the world. And who can recall the past ten vice-presidents of the United States?

Solomon draws a conclusion on this issue also, writing:

Then I became great and increased more than all who preceded me in Jerusalem. My wisdom also stood by me. . . . Then I said to myself, "As is the fate of the fool, it will also befall me. Why then have I been extremely wise?" So I said to myself, "This too is vanity." For there is no lasting remembrance of the wise man as with the fool, inasmuch as in the coming days all will be forgotten. And how the wise man and the fool alike die!

Ecclesiastes 2:9, 15–16

So the things in which man tends to spend most of his time achieving, or developing, or just maintaining, soon disappear and are forgotten. But there is one area which does not pass away—one part of man which continues to exist into the future life. And that is his spirit.

Man's spirit alone is eternal.   One of these days you will be staring death in the face. And when that happens, everything but your spirit will remain behind. All that you have worked for, all of the money in your bank, your reputation, success, and even future potential, stays here on planet earth. Solomon speaks of the last moment on earth, saying, "Then the dust will return to the earth as it was, and the spirit will return to God who gave it" (v. 12:7).

A few years ago, I saw a young man on television who had set up an elaborate display of dominos. The moment had arrived when he was about to push the first domino, which would trigger the other couple of thousand dominos in the display. It was an incredible sight. Within a little over a minute, the entire display was lying on its side. It was classy. It excited the emotions—but it was over so quickly. Later when the young man was interviewed, he was asked how long it took him to set up the display, to which he replied, "About five to six hours." I thought, *What a waste of time and energy. All of that input for a fleeting moment.*

That is typical of man's priority and value systems. Things which are temporal and fleeting receive his greatest amount of time and energy. Those things which are eternal, however, usually receive the leftover time and energy. And that is foolish.

God Is the Ultimate Source of Everything

Whatever man strives for today, he can receive from the Ultimate Source. That is why it is foolish to neglect using time in developing one's spiritual life.

God is the ultimate source of wisdom.

Men are always seeking for greater wisdom, but they usually bypass the Ultimate Source of wisdom. The Scriptures clearly point this direction. They reveal, "The fear of the Lord is the beginning of wisdom, and the knowledge of the Holy One is understanding" (Prov. 9:10). But what has man done with this tremendous resource at his fingertips? Ignored it! "For even though they knew God, they did not honor Him as God, or give thanks; but they became futile in their speculations, and their foolish heart was darkened. Professing to be wise, they became fools" (Rom. 1:21–22).

Since God's wisdom resides in His Word, it is imperative to know what He has revealed, but even many Christians ignore a regular time reading and studying the Scriptures. Therefore, many of their decisions are foolish, because they've not consulted the Ultimate Source of wisdom.

God is the ultimate source for fame.

Man consumes a lot of time promoting himself in the eyes of the world. Some will lie and cheat to get ahead. Others will use more drastic measures to achieve fame. A lot of that time could be better used, devoting oneself to the One who is able to promote and also able to demote.

The great king of Babylon, Nebuchadnezzar, learned this lesson the hard way. One night he was reflecting on his great achievements. He queried:

". . . Is this not Babylon the great, which I myself have built as a royal residence by the might of my power and for the glory of my majesty?" While the word was in the king's mouth, a voice came from heaven, saying, "King Nebuchadnezzar, to you it is declared: sovereignty has been removed from you, and you will be driven away from mankind, and your dwelling place will be with the beasts of the field. You will be given grass to eat like cattle, and seven periods of time will pass over you, until you recognize that the Most High is ruler over the realm of mankind, and bestows it on whomever He wishes." Immediately the word concerning Nebuchadnezzar was fulfilled; and he was driven away from mankind and began eating grass like cattle, and his body was drenched with the dew of heaven, until his hair had grown like eagles' feathers and his nails like birds' claws.

"But at the end of that period I, Nebuchadnezzar, raised my eyes toward heaven, and my reason returned to me, and I blessed the Most High and praised and honored Him who lives forever; for His dominion is an everlasting dominion, and His kingdom endures from generation to generation. And all the inhabitants of the earth are accounted as nothing, but He does according to His will in the host of heaven and among the inhabitants of earth; and no one can ward off His hand or say to Him, 'What has thou done?' "

Daniel 4:30–35

God is He who exalts one and puts down another. Man's responsibility is to spend time with God, and develop the inner man. Then God can open the right doors at the right time. Or as Peter puts it, "Humble yourselves, therefore, under the mighty hand of God, that He may exalt you at the proper time" (1 Peter 5:6).

God is also the ultimate source of money.

Many individuals are persuaded that making money is completely dependent on one's ability and wisdom concerning finances. God is seldom ever considered. But contrary to much popular thinking, God is both the Ultimate Source of financial success, as well as the One to whom all men are responsible as to how they manage their money.

God is the ultimate source for financial success. James warns those who make financial plans without God:

Come now, you who say, "Today or tomorrow, we shall go to such and such a city, and spend a year there and engage in business and make a profit." Yet you do not know what your life will be like tomorrow. You are just a vapor that appears for a little while and then vanishes away. Instead, you ought to say, "If the Lord wills, we shall live and also do this or that."

James 4:13–15

Furthermore, Moses warned the Israelites not to forget the One who allowed them to become wealthy:

"When you have eaten and are satisfied, you shall bless the Lord your God for the good land which *He has given you*. . . . Otherwise, you may say in your heart, 'My power and the strength of my hand made me this wealth.' But you shall remember the Lord your God, for it is He who is giving you power to make wealth. . . ."

Deuteronomy 8:10, 17–18 (*italics added*)

God is the one to whom you are accountable as to how you handle money. The amount of money you possess is not as important as how you manage what you have. In the parable of the talents, the master gave one man five talents, another two, and another, one, each according to his own ability. According to biblical measurements, a talent was one-thousand dollars in silver content, but much more valuable in buying power. Each man was held accountable for what he did with what he had. The master never expected the one-talent man to produce what the five-talent man accomplished; but he *did* expect the man to use his one talent properly.

However, when the man hid his talent, he was rebuked by his master, ". . . You wicked, lazy slave, you knew that I reap where I did not sow, and gather where I scattered no seed? Then you ought to have put *my money* in the bank, and on my arrival I would have received *my* money back with interest" (Matt. 25:26–27, *italics added*).

The person who neglects God with his money, and spends it all on himself, is called a fool by God. "And I will say to my soul, 'Soul, you have many goods laid up for many years to come; take your ease, eat, drink and be merry.' But God said to him, 'You fool! This very night your soul is required of you; and now who will own what you have prepared?' So is the man who lays up treasure for himself, and is not rich toward God" (Luke 12:19–21).

Yes, God is the Ultimate Source of wisdom, fame, and money—and life itself.

God is also the ultimate source of life.

Man often tends to think of himself as the major life source. As the anxious father-to-be waits in the fathers' room at the hospital, he shows signs of worry, frustration, and even fear. When the nurse walks into that room and announces, "Mr. Jones, you have a son," all of the anxiety evaporates into thin air, and a feeling of euphoria fills his body. He is so proud of what he was able to accomplish. He can't wait to be congratulated down at the office. His masculinity has been enhanced with the birth of his firstborn son. He wants everyone to know, "Look what *I* did."

Man merely continues what God started years ago. God created life. Man merely passes that life on to another generation. God has given us physical life, but He also offers an abundant life for the present and eternal life for the future.

Jesus said, " '. . . I came that they might have life, and might have it abundantly' " (John 10:10). He also said, " 'Truly, truly, I say to you, he who hears My word, and believes Him who sent Me, has eternal life, and does not come into judgment, but has passed out of death into life' " (John 5:24).

Now if man's spiritual life alone is eternal, it is foolish to spend so much of one's time on the physical life, or acquiring money, reaching company goals, or achieving fame. And if God is the Ultimate Source of everything, including wisdom, position in life, money, and life style, it's foolish to neglect fellowship with Him.

Think for a moment. Does God get your leftover time, or

your prime time? Are you investing the greatest amount of your time and energy in things which will fade away and be left behind at death, or do you invest quality time in eternal value?

What Happens When Man Neglects Time with God?

Having looked at the reasons why it's foolish to neglect time with God, consider now what happens when God is put on the back burner until we need Him for some unexpected emergency. There are three possible results.

An individual will remain a natural man, an immature believer, or backslide into carnality. Let's look at these three spiritual conditions more closely.

He may be a "natural man."

The term *natural* comes from the Greek *Psuchikos,* which means "belonging to the soul." The words *psyche, psychology, psychiatry,* and *psychosis* all come from this term. When it's used to describe a spiritual condition of man, it denotes the life of the natural world, and whatever belongs to it, in contrast to the supernatural world. In their Greek lexicon, Arndt and Gingrich describe it as "an unspiritual man, one who lives on the purely material plane, without being touched by the Spirit of God." Look at the following characteristics of this person.

He does not accept anything of the Holy Spirit. "But a natural man does not accept the things of the Spirit of God; for they are foolishness to him . . ." (1 Cor. 2:14). The word translated "foolish" is the Greek *mōria,* from which we derive our English word *moron.* The supernatural world seems moronic. "Nobody in his right mind would believe those stories in the Bible. They are just a bunch of myths," according to the opinion of the natural man. Or perhaps this person accepts the Bible as a religious book containing many good values, but too old-fashioned to take seriously for today's culture.

The natural man is the individual who doesn't mind a little bit of religion, but he does not want it to become personal. He sees no value or necessity of repentance, or admission of sin, or of accepting Jesus Christ as personal Savior. God is basically irrelevant to him.

He cannot understand spiritual truth. "And he cannot understand them, because they are spiritually appraised." The phrase *cannot understand* means exactly that. He is not equipped to comprehend spiritual reality. According to Scripture, he is physically and mentally alive, but spiritually dead: "And you were dead in your trespasses and sins" (Eph. 2:1). That's why Jesus described salvation as a passage out of death into life (John 5:24).

A few months ago, I bought one of those new FM headsets, which I use for jogging. It helps me keep my mind off the tiredness which can result from running. I usually leave my house tuned in to an easy-listening station. But if I begin to feel the tiredness penetrating my body, I switch to some toe-tapping music to bring me on home. The other day I took this nice headset on a short three-mile jaunt, but when I had gone only half the distance, it stopped playing. I couldn't even get a grunt out of it. My expensive toy had just given up the ghost. It looked just as good as it did the day I bought it. It still had all the buttons to push for station selection, but it was of absolutely no value to me at that point. So I took the set off my head and carried it with me for the rest of the distance. The problem wasn't hard to detect. The batteries had died. Though it was the only part of the headset that wasn't seen, it was the source which gave my headset life.

You see, even though there were invisible radio signals all around me, and even though my headset was designed to receive those signals from the air and transmit them into sound, my headset did not have the capacity to do what it was designed to do. Its batteries were dead.

In much the same way, man was designed by God to fellowship with Him. He was designed to receive and decipher spiritual truth. But when man sinned against God, His spirit died. Therefore, he cannot receive and understand the things of God's Spirit.

What, therefore, does the natural man need? He desperately needs to have his spirit brought to life. And until that miracle takes place, he will never be able to fulfill what God designed him to accomplish—know and accept the things of God.

Suppose you have already taken the step of having received Jesus Christ as your personal Savior, and for a while you understood spiritual things. You even enjoyed reading the Bible. You enjoyed fellowship with God's people. But over the years, you've allowed other things to steal your time with God. Today, you spend little time with Him, because of busyness with other things. You would probably qualify as a Christian who has never really made much spiritual progress in your life. You may be at a spiritual stalemate. Think for a moment about this spiritual condition.

He may remain an immature Christian.

Paul writes, "And I, brethren, could not speak to you as to spiritual men, but as to men of flesh, as to babes in Christ" (1 Cor. 3:1). The apostle selects a special word to describe the immature condition. The Greeks called it *sarkinos,* meaning "to make no progress in one's spiritual life"; "content to remain where one is." This individual has been a Christian for several years, but has made little progress in his spiritual life. In fact, he may have regressed in his desire to know more about God, as well as in his ability to understand the things of God.

Too often there is a wide gap between what one ought to be and what he is. The person who studied the piano for ten years ought to be able to play his piano. And if he cannot, you wonder what he was doing with the money his mother gave him for piano lessons!

The immature believer in Scripture is not so much the new Christian, as he is an older Christian, content to remain ignorant of spiritual things. The writer to the Hebrews reprimands his readers for their immaturity. He chides, "Concerning him we have much to say, and it is hard to explain, since you have become dull of hearing" (Heb. 5:11). Notice that these people became dull of hearing, which implies that at one time they enjoyed learning about spiritual things. They have regressed in their spiritual journey. The writer continues, "For though by this time you ought to be teachers, you have need again for someone to teach you the elementary principles of the oracles of God, and you have come to need milk and not solid food" (v. 12).

Time has passed. Enough time for these readers to have developed a firm understanding of the Scriptures. In fact, they should be reproducing men and women of like faith. Instead of teaching others, however, they need to go back to the *ABCs* of the Christian life. They cannot grasp deep truth.

He continues his rebuke, "For every one who partakes only of milk is not accustomed to the word of righteousness, for he is a babe. But solid food is for the mature, who because of practice have their senses trained to discern good and evil" (Heb. 5:13–14). Two observations are worth considering. First, the immature is not accustomed to the word of righteousness. You become accustomed to something by working with it. A new job, a new school, or a new location takes time for adjustment. Some people never adjust, because they make no effort to adjust. Even after years of living at the same place, they may never adjust to their surroundings.

Likewise, when a person does not spend time with God, he will not become accustomed to spiritual things. He will always feel on edge or uncomfortable, when others show their excitement and interest in spiritual growth.

A second observation is that the mature become that way by practice and training. A musician will never become a skilled artist, unless he practices several hours each day. An athlete will not reach his capacity, unless he is willing to go through many painful practice sessions. And a Christian will never really grow up spiritually, unless he is willing to pay the price of carving out time for God from his busy schedule.

You may be neither in the natural-stage category nor the immature level. Consider the third spiritual condition: the carnal man.

The carnal Christian may be a backslider.

The apostle Paul places the Corinthian believers in this category saying, "I gave you milk to drink, not solid food; for you were not yet able to receive it. Indeed, even now you are not yet able, for you are still *fleshly*. For since there is jealousy and strife among you, are you not *fleshly*, and are you not walking like mere men?" (1 Cor. 3:2–3, *italics added*). The word selected by Paul to describe this spiritual condition is very similar to what he used to describe the immature. However, there is the difference of one letter. The immature is a *sarkinos* (sarkinos), while the carnal man is a *sarkikos* (sarkikos). It means "having the nature of flesh, that is, sensual, controlled by animal appetites, governed by human nature, instead of by the Spirit of God."

Whereas the immature individual is making no spiritual progress and is content to remain immature, the carnal believer allows his lower nature to control him. He may have developed a fairly mature spiritual life over the years, but temptation has lured him away from God, and he is living a disobedient life, controlled by his appetites and not by God's Holy Spirit.

The carnal Christian is difficult to distinguish from a natural man who doesn't even profess Christianity. When people get what he thinks he deserves, he is filled with envy and jealousy. His decision making doesn't include God. In fact, he'd rather that God not interfere with his plans. He sees life from a self-centered perspective and uses worldly wisdom to advance himself in life.

He would see nothing wrong living together with the opposite sex, since many of his friends accept the practice. He doesn't mind using people for his own ends. He feels that he has a right to sow discord, if he can get enough people to agree with him. Using business "ethics," even though they conflict with biblical ethics, doesn't bother him a bit.

The carnal believer wants no authority over him. No rules or regulations. That would be interpreted as an invasion of his rights. And above everything else, the carnal believer has little time for God. He may get involved in church activity, but he will not take the time to develop his spiritual life with the Lord.

Conclusion

As you evaluate your present spiritual life with either *the natural man, the immature believer,* or *the carnal Christian,* do you see similarities or differences? The following evaluation may help you decide where you are with God at this moment.

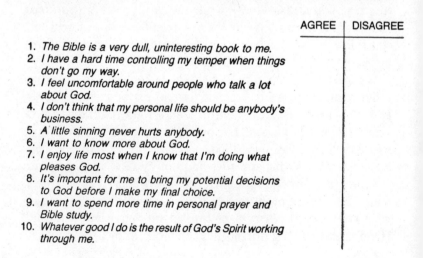

	AGREE	DISAGREE
1. The Bible is a very dull, uninteresting book to me.		
2. I have a hard time controlling my temper when things don't go my way.		
3. I feel uncomfortable around people who talk a lot about God.		
4. I don't think that my personal life should be anybody's business.		
5. A little sinning never hurts anybody.		
6. I want to know more about God.		
7. I enjoy life most when I know that I'm doing what pleases God.		
8. It's important for me to bring my potential decisions to God before I make my final choice.		
9. I want to spend more time in personal prayer and Bible study.		
10. Whatever good I do is the result of God's Spirit working through me.		

If you truthfully disagree with the first five questions, and agree with the last five, you are probably neither a natural man, an immature believer, nor a carnal Christian. But if you agree with any of the first five and disagree with any of the last five statements, you need to make some important spiritual decisions. Perhaps the two major questions you should ask yourself are:

1. On what basis do I expect to get into heaven?
2. Who will I allow to control my life?

15

Man's Greatest Use of Time— The Benefits

Introduction

In the last chapter you learned that man's greatest neglect of time is that time spent developing his spiritual life. In spite of the fact that his spirit alone is eternal, and even though God is the Ultimate Resource for everything, man continues to spend most of his time and energy on things which are temporal and will soon fade.

You also discovered that as man neglects making time for God, he will either continue through life as a natural man, without Christ; or as an immature believer who has failed to grow spiritually; or as a carnal Christian who is living under the control of the old nature.

That's the bad news. But this chapter will bring you the good news—the benefits of spending time with God. If man's greatest neglect of time is not spending it to develop his spiritual life, then his greatest use of time is to set aside a specific period each day for God.

Though the blessings resulting from your time with God will be many, for the sake of brevity let's concentrate on five of those benefits. The first four will be covered briefly. Then we will concentrate on the last one.

You Will Be Able to Refresh Your Soul

How often have you felt drained from either physical or emotional stress? Or perhaps you've received some very discouraging news, and you feel like throwing in the towel. When these circumstances prevail, you may choose either to have a private pity party, or you may decide to talk to God about the matter.

The prophet Isaiah encourages you to choose the latter when he writes, "Yet those who wait for the Lord will gain new strength; they will mount up with wings like eagles, they will run and not get tired, they will walk and not become weary" (Isa. 40:31).

There is something wonderfully refreshing when you pour out your heart and tell God what's on your mind. He accepts your complaints, disagreements, and even anger. After you are finished unloading, you feel like the athlete who suddenly gets his second wind, and goes on to complete the race as a winner.

God is the refreshing water for the thirsty soul. The psalmist describes his own thirst for God during time of distress with these words, "As the deer pants for the water brooks, so my soul pants for Thee, O God. My soul thirsts for God, for the living God; when shall I come and appear before God?" (Ps. 42:1–2).

David writes about his own experience with God, describing Him as One "who satisfies your years with good things, so that your youth is renewed like the eagle" (Ps. 103:5).

God is the Great Refresher and the One who satisfies, not only with renewed courage and strength, but also with a new perspective. And that brings us to the second great benefit of being with God.

You Will Gain a New Perspective toward Life

Have you ever wondered what an ant's world must be like? Everything in life must seem like one gigantic problem. Yet as human beings, our viewpoints are about at the same level in comparison with God's perspective. Often we can't see beyond our own ambitions. We have a tendency to evaluate everything in relation to how it affects us. However, we cannot predict the future with any degree of accuracy, nor can we even guarantee that we will be around tomorrow. So what we see for the present or future may have little to do with reality. Therefore, we need to evaluate circumstances through God's eyes and His plans.

Psalm 73 is an excellent example of one man's change of perspective. The psalmist was having difficulty over the fact that the wicked seemed to be prospering while the righteous, such as himself, were experiencing a lot of difficulty in life. The first sixteen verses record his complaint. Listen to several excerpts: "Surely God is good to Israel, to those who are pure in heart! But as for me, my feet came close to stumbling; for I was envious of the arrogant, as I saw the prosperity of the wicked" (Ps. 73:1–3).

After describing how nice the wicked have it, he begins to feel sorry for himself. "Behold, these are the wicked; and always at ease, they have increased in wealth. Surely in vain I have kept my heart pure, and washed my hands in innocence; for I have been stricken all day long, and chastened every morning. . . . When I pondered to understand this, it was troublesome in my sight" (vv. 12–14, 16).

It reminds me of some Christians whose friends are enjoying life and seem to be getting away with a lot of things that are wrong. They question, "Is the Christian life really worth it?"

Notice the pivotal verse, which reveals the change in his perspective. He was troubled, "*Until* I came into the sanctuary of God; then I perceived their end" (v. 17, *italics added*). That's what makes the difference—time with God.

Once he gained a new perspective and saw things as they really were, rather than as they first appeared, he reconfirmed his faith in God. He continues, "Nevertheless I am continually with Thee; Thou hast taken hold of my right hand. With Thy counsel Thou wilt guide me, and afterward receive me to glory. . . . But as for me, the nearness of God is my good; I have made the Lord God my refuge, that I may tell of all Thy works" (vv. 23–24, 28).

For a trusting child, the nearness of his parents is his good, but for the rebellious of heart, that nearness of parental authority is an albatross around his neck.

During the past few months, I found myself doing a lot of soul searching. It became obvious that some of the goals which I previously set were unattainable at this point. I began to question my ability, my gifts, my direction, and my future. I would change my opinion about specific issues as often as a mother changes her infant's diapers. I felt confused and frustrated.

But then I decided to spend more time with God during my regular quiet time. I read more of the Scriptures and allowed the Holy Spirit to impress His truth upon my mind. I stopped concerning myself with the future and began to focus on what God wanted to teach me in the present. In the process, I not only experienced a real refreshing of my soul, but also a new perspective of life itself. Today I see more clearly because God removed the veil of anxiety and confusion from my clouded vision.

If you are finding it difficult to accept a specific circumstance in which you find yourself, perhaps a new look at it would help—a look from God's view.

You Will Experience Opportunities Which Can Be Acquired No Other Way

This is a third benefit from spending time with God. Either prayer is a powerful tool to accomplish the impossible, or it is just a farce, or a religious crutch to which we turn when nothing else seems to work. God challenged Israel to try prayer and watch some exciting changes take place. He spoke through the prophet Jeremiah, " 'Call to Me, and I will answer you, and I will tell you great and mighty things, which you do not know' " (Jer. 33:3).

God always works according to a predesigned plan. For instance, He informed His people about His plan for them: " 'For I know the plans that I have for you,' declares the Lord, 'plans for welfare and not for calamity to give you a future and a hope. Then you will call upon Me and come and pray to Me, and I will listen to you' " (Jer. 29:11). Knowing that God does have a plan for your life, why not consult Him about that plan and ask Him to open doors which no one else can open?

I never cease to be amazed by the doors of opportunity which God has opened for me and my family. At the same time, I've opened a few doors myself, only to regret those decisions later. I am learning to leave the keys with Him and let Him do the unlocking and locking.

Many doors of opportunity are like the doors on a safe vault. The lock is timed to open at a certain hour. All of the pushing and screaming and kicking won't budge it until it's time. Then at the right moment, the lock unlocks and the doors open easily.

God first informed Abram that he would possess a land for his descendants when Abram was seventy-five years old. However, ten years passed, and he still did not have his first child, let alone "many descendants." So he and Sarai panicked and opened the door thirteen years before God's scheduled day. A lot of people have suffered since, for from that decision to take matters into their own hands, centuries of conflict have arisen between the Arab, who came from Ishmael, and the Jew, who descended from Abraham.

God has His own timer set for these doors. If we blast our way through, we may blow the opportunity permanently. That's why the psalmist encouraged his readers, "Wait for the Lord; be strong, and let your heart take courage; yes, wait for the Lord" (Ps. 27:14). And again, "Wait for the Lord, and keep His way, and He will exalt you to inherit the land; when the wicked are cut off, you will see it" (Ps. 37:34).

You Will Come to Know God on an Intimate Basis

This is a fourth direct benefit of taking the time to be with God each day. I know quite a number of people on a friendship basis, but only a few do I know intimately, because intimacy is the result of mutual trust. That takes time to develop. Some people share themselves indiscriminately with others, but this usually results in rejection by those who don't want to hear any more about their problems.

Intimacy, on the other hand, is selective. It seeks out those who truly care. It searches also for those who have the ability to deal with the problem. When it finds a caring person who can help, it shares the burden.

God is that able and caring One who asks us to come to Him and to trust Him with our hurts, desires, and fears. It was Jesus who said, " 'Come to Me, all who are weary and heavy laden, and I will give you rest' " (Matt. 11:28). The apostle Peter added, "Casting all your anxiety upon Him, because He cares for you" (1 Peter 5:7). The Lord offers intimacy, but you alone can bring it to pass by spending the necessary time with Him.

Now consider the fifth benefit of using your time with God. (This I want to explore in greater detail.)

You Will Advance toward Spiritual Maturity

From the negative perspective, the Scriptures categorize mankind as a natural man, an immature believer, or a carnal Christian—but the Bible also describes individuals from a positive posture, which includes the spiritual babe in Christ, the spiritual Christian, and the spiritually mature believer.

Observe first the babe in Christ.

The apostle Paul makes reference to the babe in Christ when he rebukes the immature Christians at Corinth for not growing spiritually as they should, "And I, brethren, could not speak to you as to spiritual men, but as to men of flesh, as to *babes in Christ*" (1 Cor. 3:1, *italics added*). Notice that Paul does not call the Corinthians babes in Christ. He says that they are behaving in an immature way—the type of behavior you would expect from one who has been a Christian for a short time.

There is nothing wrong with being a babe in Christ. Everyone who has experienced the new birth has been a babe in Christ. That is phase one of the Christian life. Whether an individual comes to Christ at the age of five or fifty, he must go through the "babe" stage. The Corinthians never advanced beyond that stage, so they were like spiritual grown-ups walking around in messy diapers.

What then characterizes babes in Christ? Like physical babies, the spiritual babe has a healthy appetite; needs someone to care for him; is limited in his ability to handle responsibility; and acts childish on occasion.

A healthy but limited appetite. The newborn infant has a very simple life style. He eats, sleeps, and cries for more to eat. The apostle Peter refers to the newborn in Christ by saying, "like newborn babes, long for the pure milk of the word, that by it you may grow in respect to salvation, if you have tasted the kindness of the Lord" (1 Peter 2:2–3).

It's always exciting to observe the new Christian, as he comes to realize what God has done for him. He wants to know more about God. He develops an insatiable interest in how God has equipped him to function in life. He hears about God's plan for man's future history and immediately wants to know how it will affect his life. Just as a young child asks, "What's this? What's that?" so the newborn Christian has a very inquisitive mind. Another characteristic of the new believer is his need for someone to care for him.

Vulnerability.   Time and again the New Testament warns the novice in the faith about those who would love to ruin that faith. Just as an infant cannot care for himself, the new believer needs protection. Paul warned the elders of Ephesus: "Be on guard for yourselves and for all the flock, among which the Holy Spirit has made you overseers, to shepherd the church of God which He purchased with His own blood. I know that after my departure, savage wolves will come in among you, not sparing the flock" (Acts 20:28–29). Now if mature elders have to be alert, so that they don't fall into the hands of unsound doctrine, how much more new believers. Just as the lions of the jungle prey on the young and the sick, so does the Enemy prowl like a roaring lion seeking to devour the young and the weak in the faith. Another characteristic concerns his ability to handle responsibility.

A limited ability to handle responsibility.   One of the greatest disservices that we can do to the new believer is to give him too much responsibility too soon. The normal pattern after a person comes to Christ is to saddle him with enormous responsibility, because of the scarcity of workers in the church. Many churches plug new converts into teaching responsibilities, committee meetings, or even into the governing board of the church.

Recognizing the danger of giving a new Christian too much responsibility too soon, Paul warns Timothy that he should never place a babe in Christ into the position of elder, "And *not a new convert,* lest he become conceited and fall into the condemnation incurred by the devil" (1 Tim. 3:6, *italics added*). Likewise, when it comes to the office of deacon, Paul writes, "And let these *first be tested;* then let them serve as deacons if they are beyond reproach" (v. 10, *italics added*). In contrast, when recommending Timothy to the Philippian church as a mature believer, the apostle writes, "But you know of his *proven worth* that he served with me in the furtherance of the gospel like a child serving his father" (Phil. 2:22, *italics added*).

This is not to say that the new believer should be given no responsibility, but he needs to be under the tutelage of a more mature believer. Whether he joins the choir, ushers in the worship service, or helps in the church nursery, he needs a lot of tender, loving care.

However, there is one responsibility in which new believers often excel beyond many older Christians—evangelism. The Gospel of Luke records such an example. As the account unfolds, Jesus is calling a tax collector to follow Him. Luke records, "And after that He went out, and noticed a tax-gatherer named Levi, sitting in the tax office, and He said to him, 'Follow me.' And he left everything behind, and rose up and began to follow Him" (Luke 5:27–28). At this point, Levi (better known as Matthew) had probably just come into a personal relationship with Christ. A new convert. Without hesitation, the first thing he wanted to do was to introduce his friends to Jesus. "And Levi gave a big reception for Him in his house; and there was a great crowd of tax-gatherers and other people who were reclining at table with them" (v. 29). It is interesting that not one religious leader was invited. No Pharisee or priest. Why? Because Levi wanted his friends to meet a Man who had just changed his life. And the only friends Levi had were sinners and other tax collectors.

Dr. Peter Wagner, vice-president of the Fuller Evangelistic Association, believes that the greatest potential for an evangelistic impact is to combine those mature believers who have the gift of evangelism with new converts who have the zeal and a host of unsaved friends. He writes, "It seems to me, therefore, that the strongest kind of mobilization for evangelism in a church is to combine those 10 percent of the mature Christians who do have the gift of evangelist with the new converts who have a role of witness and to introduce their friends and relatives to Jesus Christ through that kind of teamwork" (*Your Spiritual Gifts Can Help Your Church Grow*, p. 187).

New believers need to get involved in serving the Lord, but they should only be given as much as they can handle successfully.

There is one other character trait of the young believer, which should be mentioned, and that is his tendency to get into trouble.

A tendency to act childishly.   A child by nature is self-centered. He wants what he wants when he wants it. It is not the nature of a child to be thinking about others. He needs to learn how to share. He needs to learn the importance of treating others as he himself wants to be treated.

Paul relates his own childhood experiences writing, "When I was a child, I used to speak as a child, think as a child, reason as a child; when I became a man, I did away with childish things" (1 Cor. 13:11). So it's not unusual for a new believer to think and speak from a self-interest perspective. Therefore, when an individual comes into a personal relationship with Christ, he will experience times when he may release a few choice words from an old vocabulary when angry. He may feel that he has to shade the truth in order to get his way. He may criticize others who receive more attention than himself, or decide to leave the church, because no one seems to care about him. He is often more interested in what people can do for him, rather than he is in what he can do for others. He needs to be taught the new life and observe it modeled before him by mature believers. As he spends time with God, he will begin to move through this phase of spiritual development into the second stage.

The next stage is that of the spiritual believer.

This individual is between the babe and the mature believer in his spiritual development. The apostle John would call him a young man. He writes:

I am writing to you, little children, because your sins are forgiven you for His name's sake. I am writing to you, fathers, because you know Him who has been from the beginning. I am writing to you, *young men,* because you have overcome the evil one. I have written to you, children, because you know the Father. I have written to you, fathers, because you know Him who has been from the beginning. I have written to you, *young men,* because you are strong, and the Word of God abides in you, and you have overcome the evil one.

1 John 2:12–14 (*italics added*)

Paul also writes of this second stage of growth saying, "But he who is *spiritual* appraises all things, yet he himself is appraised by no man" (1 Cor. 2:15, *italics added*).

The word used in the passage is *Pneumatikos,* meaning "pertaining to the spirit." He is one who possesses the Holy Spirit and who allows God's Spirit to control him. Notice the following qualities which characterize his life.

He can discern spiritual truth. Remember the natural man neither receives nor can he understand spiritual truth. The immature believer has become dull of hearing spiritual truth. The carnal Christian refuses to apply spiritual truth. The babe in Christ can digest the basics of spiritual truth, but the *spiritual believer* maintains a regular, balanced diet of truth (1 Cor. 2:15). He examines the Word and is able to understand what it says, and how it applies to his life. He follows the exhortation which Paul gives to Timothy, "Be diligent to present yourself approved to God as a workman who does not need to be ashamed, handling accurately the word of truth" (2 Tim. 2:15). But he not only has the ability to handle God's Word accurately, he also walks under the control of God's Holy Spirit.

He lives under the authority of God's Holy Spirit. The spiritual believer is spiritual in that his ambitions in life, his thoughts, and his motivation grow out of his sensitivity and availability to God's Spirit. He experiences what Paul describes to the Philippians, "for it is God who is at work in you, both to will and to work for His good pleasure" (Phil. 2:13). He lives as one who is filled with the Holy Spirit (Eph. 5:18). He refuses to allow the old nature to run his life, so he does not behave like the natural man, the immature believer, or the carnal Christian, because he walks by means of the Holy Spirit (Gal. 5:16). This means that he makes the best use of his time (Eph. 5:16), he does not get drunk (v. 18), he fellowships with other believers (v. 19), and gives thanks continually to God (v. 20). He is willing to be in subjection to authority (v. 21).

The spiritual believer is not immune to sin, but his desire is to please God in everything that he does (Eph. 5:10). He also has a deep interest in and sensitivity to others.

He has a concern for others. Whereas the new believer is still primarily interested in what others can do for his personal growth, the spiritual believer has developed an interest in others. He lives the principle expressed in Philippians, "Do nothing from selfishness or empty conceit, but with humility of mind let each of you regard one another as more important than himself; do not merely look out for your own personal interests, but also for the interests of others" (Phil. 2:3–4).

He is interested not only in another's physical or emotional needs, he also has a concern about other people's spiritual lives. That's why Paul felt free to exhort the spiritual Christian, "Brethren, even if a man is caught in any trespass, *you who are spiritual,* restore such a one in a spirit of gentleness; looking to yourself, lest you too be tempted. Bear one another's burden's and thus fulfil the law of Christ" (Gal. 6:1–2, *italics added*).

However, the spiritual stage is not the ultimate phase of growth. There is a further reach—maturity.

The spiritually mature believer has reached the ultimate phase of growth.

The word used for maturity is the Greek *Teleios*—meaning "complete" or "full grown." The apostle Paul states this as his goal for the Colossian Christian, "And we proclaim Him, admonishing every man and teaching every man with all wisdom, that we may present every man *complete* in Christ" (Col. 1:28, *italics added*). He further informs the Ephesians that God gave gifted men to the church "for the equipping of the saints for the work of service, to the building up of the body of Christ; until we all attain to the unity of faith, and of the knowledge of the Son of God, to a *mature man*, to the measure of the stature which belongs to the fulness of Christ" (Eph. 4:12–13, *italics added*).

What is a mature believer like? How does he think? What does he do? He is a spiritual believer who has developed several other qualities over the years. Some of his qualities are revealed in the Book of Colossians.

The mature believer is sensitive to God's will and guidance. ". . . we have not ceased to pray for you and to ask that you may be filled with the knowledge of His will in all spiritual wisdom and understanding" (Col. 1:9).

God's will is revealed in His Word. Therefore, the mature person has an excellent grasp of truth. He understands how it relates to contemporary life. He does not look for the loopholes. Instead, he brings his decisions and his life style under the authority and scrutiny of God's Word.

Much of my early instruction in Scripture was learned under the teaching of several laymen who were men of the Book. One man, who was in his late sixties, had taught himself Greek, and also knew how to use the Hebrew language for word studies. For years he opened his home to conduct Bible studies for any who wanted to come. He was a teacher of disciples who taught others also (2 Tim. 2:2). Another characteristic of the mature believer concerns his walk with God.

The mature believer walks worthy of God. ". . . so that you may walk in a manner worthy of the Lord, to please Him in all respects, bearing fruit in every good work, and increasing in the knowledge of God" (Col. 1:10).

This individual pleases God in the way he handles his finances; how he controls his moral life style; how he relates to the members of his family; and how he involves himself in serving God. The spiritually mature individual also bears fruit. That means that he is productive in his work. There may be periods when he is more productive than others. In fact, he may lose a few crops here and there, but his harvest record indicates much success in achieving the goals he sets.

This believer is also strong in the faith, constantly learning about the character and power of God. And he enjoys the deep truths of God's Word. The last quality focuses on his experiences with the problems of life.

The mature believer has experienced life's trials.   One not only develops maturity by reading and applying the Scriptures to life, but also by experiencing various testings. James writes, "Consider it all joy, my brethren, when you encounter various trials; knowing that the testing of your faith produces endurance. And let endurance have its perfect result, that you may be perfect and complete, lacking in nothing" (James 1:2–4).

The testing may come in the form of the loss of a loved one, financial difficulty, physical handicaps, sickness, loss of a job, or rejection by others because of your witness for Christ.

The loss of my mother when I was in college challenged my faith. I remember well the night she died. A group of fellow students gathered in my room to pray with me. Together, through the tears, we sang "How Great Thou Art." Though many questions were raised in my mind during those agonizing days before and after the funeral, God became very close and very real. It indeed was a maturing process.

Conclusion

Are you experiencing any of these benefits? If not, this would be a good time to pause for a moment of prayer. Stop your reading and take a moment to reflect on where you are with God.

Would your spiritual condition be closer to that of the natural man—the immature believer—the carnal Christian; or the babe in Christ—the spiritual believer—and the spiritually mature believer?

God's purpose for you is that you grow strong in your faith and in your knowledge of Him. And that can be accomplished only as you carve some time out of each day's schedule and spend it with God.

Now you're ready to see just how you can make this time with God become an effective tool for your spiritual development.

16

Man's Greatest Use of Time— The Essentials

Introduction

When Vince Lombardi, the eminent coach of the Green Bay Packers in the 1960s, was asked how he produced winning teams, he replied that any group of naturally endowed football athletes could win more games then they lost, if they concentrated on the fundamentals of the game—blocking, tackling, kicking, passing, pass receiving, and running.

After a close game won by his Green Bay Packers, Lombardi called a special session for Monday morning. Appearing before his players, he held a football above his head and announced, "Men, we need to review the fundamentals of the game. . . . This . . . is . . . a . . . football." One of his players replied, "That's a little fast, coach. Go over that again."

Lombardi's principle of mastering the basics is not only essential to the development of a winning football team. It applies to every major area of life, including one's spiritual life.

If I were to put my finger on any one reason why so many Christians are not winning the spiritual warfare, it's because they've never mastered the basics—an effective prayer life; the joy of discovering God's Word firsthand; a dynamic witness of one's faith in Christ; and a consistent walk with the Holy

Spirit. Failure to develop in those aspects of the Christian life guarantees defeat in the Christian life itself.

Therefore, I want to identify those basic elements, which will make your time with God an exciting and growing experience. First, we'll look at the essential characteristics, and then observe the essential ingredients for an effective quiet time with God.

The Essential Characteristics

If you are like most Christians, you have probably enjoyed time with God on many occasions. However, you also know what it's like to have a quiet time when nothing seems to gel. In fact, those times were actually a waste. Why do we experience such inconsistency during those very important moments? One possible reason is because we've neglected one of the basic qualities of a quiet time.

Solitude, as one example.

Many people attempt to have their quiet times in the house, while the kids are running back and forth, the phone is ringing, and the dog is barking. Others use their cars for an inner sanctum, but find it difficult to do anything other than develop ulcers from trying to keep their cool in heavy traffic, the honking of horns, and idiotic drivers dashing back and forth in the traffic lanes. What they are lacking is *solitude*.

After a hectic day of ministering to the multitudes, Jesus sent them away, and then put His disciples into a boat and sent them away. Finally by Himself, the Lord found solitude with His Father, "And after He had sent the multitudes away, He went up to the mountain by Himself to pray; and when it was evening, He was there alone" (Matt. 14:23). That's solitude. Just you and God. Everything else is closed out. No distractions. No interruptions.

This may seem like an impossibility to a busy person, but

it is essential if you want to mean business with God. You need full concentration when you come into His presence.

I recall how I felt the very first time I had a private meeting with Billy Graham. It was during my freshman year in college. Dr. Graham was holding a crusade at the old Madison Square Garden in New York City. About one hundred students from our school were planning to attend the crusade Saturday evening, but four of us went to New York Friday afternoon. Since Bob Marquardt and I were on the school newspaper staff, we ventured into the press room, hoping to secure passes for the press box. What a thrill it was to be sitting with reporters from the *New York Times, Time* magazine, the *Philadelphia Inquirer,* and other major news agencies. Bob had one of those old press cameras, so he and I decided to get an interview with Dr. Graham. We left our press seats and meandered through the corridors looking for his room. Suddenly a crowd of reporters emerged from around the corner, with the eminent evangelist in the middle. Without hesitation, I ran up to him, explained that I was on the staff of our school paper, and asked for an interview. He smiled and agreed to have a private interview with Bob and me after the rest of the press interviewed him.

We anxiously waited outside the room. After about twenty minutes, the press emerged from the room with their scoops and dashed to the press seats in the old Garden. Dr. Graham then came to the door, put his arms around the two of us, and ushered us into the room for a private interview. We expressed our appreciation, took a few pictures, and asked some questions. During that fifteen-minute interview, there were no interruptions. No phone calls. Billy Graham talked with us as though he had nothing else to do that evening. He knew how to make two young college students feel as though they were more important to him than the thousands of people who were already singing hymns in the Garden, awaiting his appearance.

That's how your time with God needs to be. He enjoys

the multitudes, and He is worthy to be acknowledged by all mankind. But He also enjoys those times alone with you. He opens the door and puts His arms around you, extending to you a private audience. God is in no hurry. He will not interrupt you. He will not be distracted by the wars taking place around the world. He gives you the individual attention, so why not place your full concentration on Him? Just the two of you in solitude.

Another essential characteristic of an effective quiet time is consistency.

So often our time with God is a hit-or-miss proposition. We govern ourselves by convenience rather than by *consistency*.

What is consistency? It is primarily another way of saying *self-discipline*. If you want to lose weight, you consistently need to eat properly, consuming less and exercising more. When the routine is broken, the weight returns. If you are developing a new skill, you need to be consistent in your practice. The golfer who wants to shoot in the low eighties will not achieve his goal by playing golf whenever he finds the time. He must consistently practice, working on the basics.

The two basic areas where consistency is essential are in the time and the location of your devotional period.

Be consistent in time. When do you have your quiet time with God? Any time you choose is fine with Him, but it is easier for you when the same time period is set aside, than if you wait for a convenient time.

(1) *Morning*—The psalmist wrote, "In the morning, O Lord, Thou wilt hear my voice; In the morning I will order my prayer to Thee and eagerly watch" (Ps. 5:3). But look at the time when Peter prayed.

(2) *Noon*—"And on the next day, as they were on their way, and approaching the city, Peter went up on the housetop

about the sixth hour to pray" (Acts 10:9). The sixth hour refers to noontime.

(3) *Evening*—But morning and noon are only two possible choices. You've already seen where Jesus went to His Father in the evening for a time of solitude (Matt. 14:23).

I do not imply that you can have only one audience with God each day, but what I am saying is that you should begin with a specific time and keep to it as much as is possible.

However, another area where consistency helps is not only in the time you choose, but where.

Be consistent in location. Again you may pray to God at any time and in any place, but it will be helpful if you go to the same place each day for those moments of solitude. It helps you develop the necessary discipline and that quiet place becomes very special to you.

When I was a student in college, I used a vacant dorm room for my quiet time. That way I didn't have to worry about interruptions from my roommate. Some like to use the kitchen or family room, or even the guest bedroom. Others go down to their offices early enough to be alone with God.

Whatever you choose, you should be able to feel alone with God. Close the door. Remember, you are appearing before One who is greater than any king, president, or other dignitary. If the president of the United States offered you a private audience, you'd break your neck to get there and would welcome all the privacy afforded you. Why not do the same for the King of kings?

Solitude and consistency are qualities which will greatly improve your time with God. But let's add a third character quality—variety.

Use variety in your devotions.

Some people carry consistency so far that they become bound in tradition. They feel that the only proper time to have a quiet period with God is during their particular hour; or the only proper method to use is their method. This perspective has absolutely no justification. In fact, unless one uses variety, his quiet time with God can get so quiet, he'll fall asleep!

Recently at our staff retreat, I asked our members to share what they have found to be helpful in their personal devotions. I was amazed at the variety they use. I don't believe any one of our eight staff members uses the same approach in his quiet time with God. They use a great deal of variety in their reading of Scripture and in their praying.

In reading.   Some of the staff read the Scriptures using different translations, while others will read the Bible, using a commentary to help them understand it more clearly. You might try reading one chapter from an Old Testament book and another chapter from a New Testament portion.

There are those who enjoy reading devotional books along with the Bible, while others use the Bible only. Some have found it helpful to write a paraphrase of what they've read. In other words, they put the essence of the meaning into their own words.

You also might try personalizing God's promises. Jeremiah speaks for God, promising Israel, " 'For I know the plans that I have for you,' declares the Lord, plans for welfare and not for calamity to give you a future and a hope" (Jer. 29:11). To personalize this, you could write in a notebook, "I know that God's plans for me are good. They provide a future and a hope. I will do everything possible to fit into His plans for my life."

You should also use variety when praying to God.

In praying.   This could include praying from the Scriptures themselves. For instance, take some of the prayers from the Bible and make them your own. David's prayer of confession in Psalm 51 could become yours. Or from Paul's prayer for the Colossians you might pray, "Lord, help me to discern Your will on a daily basis. Give me the desire and strength to walk in a manner worthy of being called Your child. Teach me how to please You in all respects: how I relate to my spouse, how I manage my money, and how I treat others. Make me fruitful in the tasks I perform. And help me to increase in my knowledge of You. Make me strong in the faith. Show me how to develop patience so that I don't panic or operate on my own time schedule. Give me the courage to persevere, even when I feel like giving up. And I'll constantly give You thanks for every blessing You bestow upon me. In Jesus' name, *amen"* (Col. 1:9–12).

Another approach to prayer is to take a specific topic each day and focus on it: Monday—*missions;* Tuesday—*tasks;* Wednesday—*workers;* Thursday—*thanks;* Friday—*family;* Saturday—*sinners;* Sunday—*saints.* You can use your own creative ability to make this scheme work for you.

Others have found it helpful to keep a prayer log with four columns:

1. date of request
2. request
3. answer
4. date of answer

Or one further suggestion for variety is to write a prayer letter to God. Instead of just orally verbalizing your needs or thanks, write your prayer. You may desire to keep these letters in a notebook, so that you can see the progress you're making in prayer.

You'll want to avoid sameness, because it can lead to boredom—or worse yet—legalism: the practice which carries on the form after it has lost the intent. Some people have a devotional time for the sake of completing their spiritual obligation, *but they've lost the whole purpose of being with God.*

A devotional period is not intended to be some magic formula to keep the believer out of trouble. Nor is it a duty to perform. Instead, it should be considered one of the greatest opportunities for a man or woman to ever experience—an audience with the very Creator of heaven and earth. The Landlord of this planet. The Sovereign of the universe. That should get everyone excited.

What works for you today may not be what you need tomorrow. Too much of the same thing can eventually become either boring or nauseating. The writer of Proverbs said it explicitly, "Have you found honey? Eat only what you need, lest you have it in excess and vomit it" (25:16).

Are you using solitude when you spend time with God? Are you really alone with Him? How about consistency? Is that a characteristic of your intimate periods with God? Have you learned to use a variety of methods, so that those quiet moments remain fresh, renewing your spirit? Each of these qualities should be indicative of your relationship with God. But let's move from the essential *characteristics* to the essential *ingredients* of a quiet time. We've looked briefly at the need to use Scripture and prayer, but now let's go a little deeper with those areas.

The Essential Ingredients

What should an individual actually do during his devotional period? What will help him be refreshed in spirit and renewed in perspective? What ingredients will act like spiritual vitamins to give him a healthy, growing, inner life?

The foundational ingredient is the Bible itself.

The Bible is God's greatest instrument through which He speaks to you. It's the source of information concerning His character and His works; His will and His warnings; His blessings and His curses. Everything you need to know about God is treasured within that Book. Therefore, one of the major purposes of being with God is to get to know Him better. What should you do with the Bible during those sacred moments? Begin by reading it.

Read the Scriptures systematically. Sometimes you will read one or several chapters at a time, while on other occasions you'll read entire books at one sitting, for instance, Epistles of John, Jude, 1 and 2 Peter, Philippians, Philemon, and Colossians. The purpose of reading large segments is to gain an overview of the Book.

When I was attending Bible College, we were required to read every book of the Bible we studied three times, using three different translations. Often that included books like Genesis with fifty chapters, or the Psalms with 150 chapters. When you cover that much material, don't get bogged down in detail. Look for key thoughts or impressions. Feel free to use a yellow marker or a pen, and underline verses which seem to speak directly to you. In fact, you may wish to write down some thoughts in the margin of your Bible.

I've read systematically through the entire Old Testament with this method, and I've found it to be extremely enlightening. Now I enjoy flipping through portions of the Old Testament to see what I've underlined, and I get blessed all over again.

Reading the Bible is an excellent way to gain quick thoughts for the day. However, this type of reading provides only a surface knowledge of Scripture. For greater depth, you'll have to study the Word.

Study the Scriptures carefully. Bible study was never meant to be an exclusive opportunity for the few, but instead it is the responsibility and privilege of every believer. Paul encouraged Timothy, "Be diligent to present yourself approved to God as a workman who does not need to be ashamed, handling accurately the word of truth" (2 Tim. 2:15).

The average Christian does not know how to study the Bible for himself. I believe that much of the blame lies on the shoulders of the church leaders who have failed to equip them properly. Too many pastors and teachers have neglected their responsibility to teach believers how to feed themselves spiritually. We've raised generations of spiritual infants who are solely dependent on others to teach them truth. They've not learned to feed themselves.

However, in many cases the blame must be shared by Christians, who are either too lazy, too busy with lesser things, or just too disinterested to take the time to learn.

The average Christian who invests no more time in his spiritual life than to attend a worship service once a week for spiritual nourishment, will be ill-equipped to face life's battles during the week.

Imagine what most of us would look like if we ate one meal a week! In some countries, that's about all they have to live on. The name for that problem is *starvation*. Today the churches are filled with the spiritually malnourished because Christians feed on so little spiritual food.

Because of this problem, I committed myself to God several years ago to write Bible studies which will help people study the Scriptures for themselves. I want every believer to experience the first-hand joy of personal Bible study.

If you get involved in a group Bible study, you could use part of your quiet time with God, answering the questions in the group study. If you have never really studied the Bible for yourself, it would probably be to your advantage to purchase some Bible-study materials to help you develop the skills of personal study. Another approach to the Scriptures is memorization.

Memorize the Scriptures regularly. Since I am constantly studying the Word, I don't consciously memorize specific verses as I used to. I find by going over various passages so often, the verses stay with me. Though I may not always quote them word for word, I can usually produce a good paraphrase when I want to refer to the verse.

In my earlier years as a Christian, I spent hours memorizing verses of Scripture. I'd carry memory packs with me, so that I could rehearse them in my mind during spare moments.

Some Christians will take one of their devotional periods each week to learn whole passages of Scripture. You could memorize key verses, an entire book, or specific verses on various topics such as salvation, worry, money, peace, and so forth. Once those verses are hidden in your heart, the Holy Spirit can bring them to your conscious mind during times of temptation, difficulty, or when you want to encourage others. One other use of the Scriptures during your quiet time is meditation.

Meditate on Scripture thoughtfully. You hear a lot about meditation today. The Eastern religions emphasize the practice, but usually the meditation is on everything but God. The object of one's meditation is as important as the method of meditation. The psalmist testifies, "And I shall lift up my hands to Thy commandments, which I love; and I will meditate on Thy statutes" (Ps. 119:48). But what is meant by *meditation?*

The Hebrews have two key words which are translated "meditate." The first *hâgâh.* This is a low sound, characteristic of the moaning of a dove (Isaiah 38:14) or the growling of a lion over its prey (31:4). The one who meditated in this way probably read the Scripture half outloud or pondered over it in a low voice.

David referred to this method when he wrote, "When I remember Thee on my bed, I meditate on Thee in the night watches" (Ps. 63:6). Anyone walking by the king's bedroom at night would probably have heard a muffled sound coming from the room. They would know right away that the king was meditating on His God.

The second word is the *sîyach,* meaning "to rehearse" or "to go over a matter in one's mind." The psalmist writes, "Oh how I love Thy law! It is my meditation all the day" (Ps. 119:97). The psalmist would think about God's Word and keep turning it over in his mind.

Meditating is something like working the Rubik's Cube. You look at it, turn it over and over again, until the various parts begin to make sense by fitting a color pattern. Meditating on God's Word by turning it over and over in your mind will help you to see the variety of areas in which it can be applied. You'll see a pattern of God's operation begin to emerge.

Prayer is the second essential ingredient to an effective devotional time.

Whereas God speaks to you through His Word, you speak to Him in prayer. Prayer is such a vast subject, that it's difficult to condense. But I'll attempt this task by commenting on the five major aspects of prayer. Let's begin with confession.

Confession—Not every quiet time will necessarily have a time of confession. Though the Bible tells us to confess our sins to God (1 John 1:9), it does not demand any morbid introspection. Some Christians feel guilty if they can't come up with some gross sin to confess. God holds us responsible, when we consciously sin, to agree with Him that we have sinned. He wants us to turn away from that sin and accept His forgiveness. If we are not conscious of a specific sin, we are not required to generalize.

Sometimes we have to be with people for a long time before we realize what they do or do not like. A wife may say to her husband, "I didn't know that bothered you." Or a husband to his wife, "I never realized how my joking about you offends you so much." It takes some couples years before such information surfaces. Likewise the more intimate we become with God, the more conscious we will become of sin. Attitudes and behavior, which were once acceptable in our sight, will become evident as unpleasing to God. Then we confess them as sin.

Petition—When people don't like the way something is being done, they often get up a petition of grievances. So when you come to God, you may actually have some grievances. Don't be afraid to share them with Him. He knows exactly where you are coming from anyway. However, petition also includes other requests which God wants you to bring to Him. It was Jesus who said: "Ask, and it shall be given to you; seek, and you shall find; knock, and it shall be opened to you. For every one who asks receives, and he who seeks finds, and to him who knocks it shall be opened" (Matt. 7:7–8).

Praise—A third important type of praying is expressed by the joy which flows from your heart. The Bible calls it praise. Praise is the expression of an overflowing heart. We praise our favorite football teams (when they win their games!) by telling everyone how great they are. We praise those who are successful in all areas of life, because we feel that they are worthy of the honor.

How much more is God worthy of our praise. You can praise the Lord in song as the psalmist declares, "Praise the Lord! For it is good to sing praise to our God; for it is pleasant and praise is becoming" (Psalm 147:1).

When I was a college student, I worked at Ocean Grove, New Jersey, one summer. I'd work from 3:00 to 11:00 P.M. in the drugstore, and then go down to the pier and have my devotions. It was too dark to read the Bible, but it provided a great opportunity for me to pray, meditate, and praise God in song. With the noise of the ocean waves, I was able to sing at the top of my lungs, and no one but God could hear me.

If you decide to praise God in song, you'd better make certain that you're alone, or that you have a pleasant voice, so others can enjoy the praise. You can also praise the Lord verbally by telling God how much you love Him.

Thanksgiving—And along with praise, comes a companion—thanksgiving. Sometimes in the Scriptures, thanksgiving is used interchangeably with praise. When it is used distinctively, praise usually focuses on expressing homage, admiration, and approval of God's character and works. Thanksgiving, on the other hand, is acknowledging a divine favor. You praise God whether He blesses you or not, because

He is deserving of praise. But you thank God when He specifically relates to you in a personal way.

You might praise your favorite football team for winning their game, but you probably would not thank them. However, you might thank one of the players for his autograph, because he did you a personal favor.

Likewise, you praise God that He is a powerful God. He is the Creator. He performs mighty deeds. He is worthy of your worship. However, when He shows you a personal favor and blesses you specifically, you personally thank Him. Why not write down a specific "thank you" list? Thank God for your health, your family, your salvation, your opportunities. All that He gives to you, and all that He does for you (and all that He doesn't do to you, even though you deserve it)—return with words of thanksgiving.

Confession, petition, praise, and thanksgiving are four essential parts of prayer, but there is one other aspect which needs to be included, when you spend time with God in prayer. And that is intercession.

Intercession—Intercession reveals your concern for others. Sad to say, this kind of prayer is often absent from a devotional period. Most of the apostle Paul's prayers are intercessions for others. He wrote to the Ephesians, ". . . [I] do not cease giving thanks for you, while making mention of you in my prayers" (Eph. 1:16). To the Philippians he wrote, "And this I pray, that your love may abound still more and more in real knowledge and all discernment" (Phil. 1:9).

It is interesting to note that he didn't wait until the believers became basket cases and then pleaded to God for their deliverance. He held them up in prayer, even when everything seemed to be going well for them.

If you told the average Christian that you were praying for him, he'd wonder what you found out, or if you knew something he didn't. We often ask people to pray for us when we're going through periods of great difficulty. But why wait until then? We need each other's prayers, even when everything is going well. I covet the prayers of my friends on a daily basis, not because of some great difficulty, but because I need greater growth in my spiritual life. I need God's wisdom for decision making; His courage to do what must be done; His patience to wait for His timing; His love to flow through me to others; and His strength to resist the daily temptations of life.

Conclusion

The basics. You can't get much more basic than to focus on the Scriptures and prayer during your quiet time with God. Even though most of this information is not new, the important question which demands a response from you is "to what degree are you mastering these basics?"

Sometimes I feel like I need to adopt Vince Lombardi's method when he held up the football and said, "Gentlemen, this is a football." I feel that I need to say, "Reader, this is a Bible—master it." "And this is prayer—practice it."

If you will take time each day out of your busy schedule and allow God to communicate to you through His Word, and then communicate to Him through prayer, your quiet time will produce the benefits you read about in the previous chapter.

Time with God—that's the greatest way to spend your time.

Bibliography

"As Americans Cope with the Changing Population." *U.S. News & World Report.* August 9, 1982.

Brown, Mary (ed.). "The Ingredients of a Good Friendship." *Psychology Today.* October, 1979.

Clarkson, Margaret. *So You're Single.* Wheaton: Shaw Publishers, 1978.

Dayton, Edward R. *Tools for Time Management.* Grand Rapids: Zondervan Publishing House, 1974.

Dayton, Ed and Engstrom, Ted. *Strategy for Leadership.* Old Tappan, NJ: Fleming H. Revell Company, 1979.

Dobson, Dr. James. *Dr. Dobson Answers Your Questions.* Wheaton: Tyndale House Publishers, Inc., 1982.

Dobson, Dr. James. *Hide or Seek.* Old Tappan, NJ: Fleming H. Revell Company, 1974.

Engstrom, Dr. Ted. "Time For Things That Matter." *Leadership Magazine.* Carol Stream, IL: Christianity Today, Inc., Spring 1982.

Gherman, Dr. E. M. *Stress and the Bottom Line.* New York: Amacom, 1981.

Hansel, Tim. *When I Relax I Feel Guilty.* Elgin, IL: David C. Cook Publishing Company, 1979.

Johnson, James L. *Loneliness Is Not Forever.* Chicago: Moody Press, 1979.

King, Pat. *How Do You Find the Time.* Lynnwood, WA: Aglow Publications, 1975.

LaHaye, Tim and Bev. *Spirit-Controlled Family Living.* Old Tappan, NJ: Fleming H. Revell Company, 1978.

Lakein, Alan. *How to Get Control of Your Time and Your Life.* New York: New American Library, Inc., 1973.

Landorf, Joyce. *Tough and Tender.* Old Tappan, NJ: Fleming H. Revell Company, 1975.

Lewis, Paul (ed.). "News For Thought." *Dads Only.* Julian, CA, March, 1981.

Lewis, Paul (ed.). "News For Thought." *Dads Only.* Julian, CA, September, 1981.

Lewis, Paul (ed.). "News For Thought." *Dads Only.* Julian, CA, October, 1981.

MacKenzie, R. Alex. *The Time Trap.* New York: McGraw-Hill Book Company, 1972.

McGinnis, Alan Loy. *The Friendship Factor.* Minneapolis: Augsburg Publishing House, 1979.

Meier, Dr. Paul D. *Christian Child-Rearing and Personality Development.* Grand Rapids: Baker Book House, 1977.

Obledo, Mario G. "Friends Can Be Good Medicine." California Department of Mental Health. Health and Welfare Agency, 1981.

Potthoff, Harvey H. *Loneliness: Understanding and Dealing with It.* Nashville: Abingdon, 1976.

Powell, John. *Why Am I Afraid to Tell You Who I Am?* Niles, IL: Argus Communications, 1969.

Rohrer, Norman B. and Sutherland, S. Philip. *Why Am I Shy?* Minneapolis: Augsburg Publishing House, 1978.

Schuller, Dr. Robert H. *Move Ahead with Possibility Thinking.* Garden City, New York: Doubleday & Company, Inc., 1967.

Schuller, Dr. Robert H. *The Peak to Peek Principle.* Garden City, New York: Doubleday & Company, Inc., 1980.

Senter, Ruth. "When You Care Too Much." *Today's Christian Woman.* Old Tappan, NJ: Fleming H. Revell Company, Fall 1982.

Smoke, Jim. *Growing Through Divorce.* Eugene, OR: Harvest House Publishers, 1976.

Speakman, Frederick B. *Love Is Something You Do.* New York: Harper & Row, 1979.

Strauss, Dr. Richard. *Confident Children and How They Grow.* Wheaton, IL: Tyndale House Publishers, 1975.

"The Superwoman Squeeze." *Newsweek.* May 19, 1980.

Swindoll, Charles R. *Strike the Original Match.* Portland: Multnomah Press, 1980.

Tanner, Ira J. *Loneliness: The Fear of Love.* New York: Harper & Row, 1974.

Wagner, C. Peter. *Your Spiritual Gifts Can Help Your Church Grow.* Glendale: Regal Books, 1979.

ABOUT THE AUTHOR

DR. RICK YOHN is the pastor of the fast-growing Evangelical Free Church of Fresno, California. He is a respected and experienced author. In addition to his writing, he has a radio program and is one of the most popular speakers of the Family Life Cassette of the Month Club. His published works include: *Character Growth: Priority for Christian Living, Discover Your Spiritual Gift and Use It, Getting Control of Your Life, God's Answers to Financial Problems, God's Answers to Life's Problems, God's Holy Spirit for Christian Living, Now That I'm a Disciple, What Every Christian Should Know about God, First Hand Joy: A Step by Step Guide to Help You Study Bible Passages on Your Own,* and *Getting Control of Your Inner Self.*

Dr. Yohn is a graduate of Dallas Theological Seminary and Talbot Theological Seminary. He and his wife, Linda, have two sons: Rick and Steve.

95035